LONESOME STRAY

by
Patrick C. Rice

AuthorHouse™ UK Ltd.
500 Avebury Boulevard
Central Milton Keynes, MK9 2BE
www.authorhouse.co.uk
Phone: 08001974150

First published by AuthorHouse 8/16/2007

ISBN: 978-1-4343-1201-3 (sc)

Printed in the United States of America
Bloomington, Indiana

This book is printed on acid-free paper.

To my family

Ghosts from the Past

Kingsley House

Travelling through the fertile farmland of England's West Midlands you come across beautiful designated areas of SSI (special scientific interest). In one such area perhaps passing strangers who come across this large country house might think we don't conform to their concept of a couple likely to reside here.

It nestles on a hillside surrounded by woodland. It's grounds, of some four green acres, softly unfolds in layers down to an unspoilt meandering river. Wild life abounds on this

1

quiet stretch of river with its rare species of fish. The area nurtures all manners of rare plants and fauna. There's my wife Jean and I Paddy living in this large six-bedroom house. She is one of five children from a mining community in Co. Durham.

Jean Aged 16

Like most children of working class families in the 1940s and 1950's she left school at fourteen to join her older sister at the local clothing factory to earn a living, later to be joined by her younger sister. Her two younger brothers had little option but join their Father in the coalmines as fourteen-year-olds. I by contrast originate from Ireland a product of the Industrial School system, where children under ten charged with wrongdoing, or orphaned were sentenced by the courts to be detained, and disposed of (in the courts words) at age sixteen. Having spent most of my childhood in two of these boys' only institutions it is hardly surprising I would ever fully integrate in the outside world. At age ten I was transferred from the custody of nuns to that of the Christian Brothers at the notorious 'Artane' Industrial School, where I underwent harsh discipline and daily work. In a strange world I soon learned to hide my past for fear of showing an ignorance of the accepted norms.

An example would be my lack of knowledge about giving and receiving cards and presents at birthdays and Christmas. In 1949 aged seventeen I left Ireland to get far away from my past and start a new life in England. Keeping all relationships at arms length for fear of embarrassment by letting slip by word or deed displaying a lack of social graces. It would be three years before I felt it safe to lower my guard a little. It was to be Jean, my inspiration, and the girl who showed me the power of love. Married in 1955 we were blessed with a son a year later followed eighteen months later in Germany by the birth of a daughter. Though born in a British Military Hospital we were refused a British Birth Certificate for the child, because I was an Irish Citizen. The Irish authorities questioned my serving in the British Forces resulting in her being registered as a German! To complete our family Karen was born in 1962. Life turned out better than ever I could ever have dreamed, living and working in different countries of Europe, the Far and Middle East. In 1974 we settled down here in the Midlands in our very own first house. Things were going blissfully well and Jean recalled the vision I had for our future. In the early years of marriage I had told her: "One day we will have a big house in the country, with a nice drive and open spaces for children to play". Looking at our newly built three bed-roomed detached house she questioned: "Is this the dream house you talked about all those years ago when we had just enough money to get by?" I told her it didn't fit the picture of my dreams. Two years later our older daughter married and our son left home. Then Shock! Horror, our young fifteen-year-old girl was knocked down and killed.

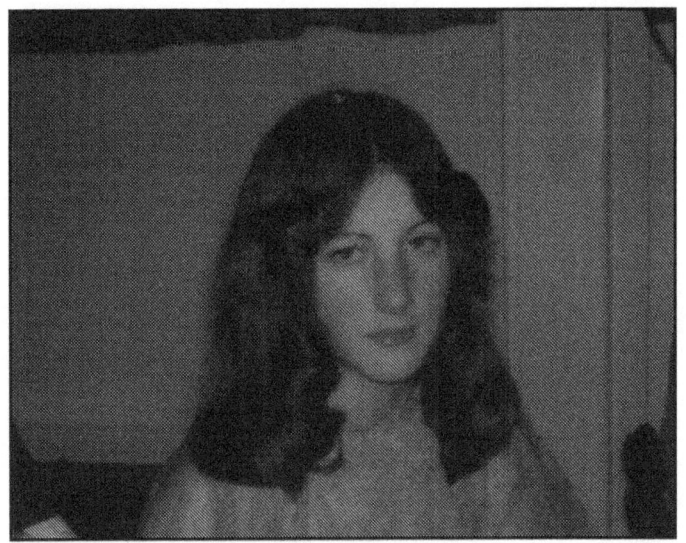

Karen aged 14

On first sight Jean expressed a lack of enthusiasm about my newly found dream home until I convinced her of its potential merits. Or maybe she just couldn't bring herself to quench my overwhelming joy at the sight of the place.

From the 19th of October '77 to the end of '78 is just a blur in my mind. Once again I thought to escape pain and heartbreak, in more senses than one. I run each day punishing my body until I dropped. I had to get away from this torturous place and try to find peace. It was late 1978 I came across this, my dream home, hidden away along a narrow snaking road shaded by an overhanging canopy of trees.

"Why would we want a big old place like this?" "Come on Jean, can you remember asking me if the house we are living in was the one I promised we'd own one day? And I told you no. Well this is it, the dream home."

Early in our marriage whilst lying in bed I talked of my determination for us to own a large country home. I had envisaged a long driveway and plenty of land for children to play and here it was. This driving ambition I held firm in spite then of being just able to make ends meet with a wife and child to support. "I still don't understand. It's far too big for just us two and what about the cottage?" "It's for our grandchildren, and as for the cottage the old lady can stay there as long as she wishes and pay you the rent"

Kingsley House 2

"But we don't have any grandchildren and you don't know we ever will." "Trust me, we will and I'll do everything in my power to make you and our future brood happy here." Within three years we managed to own it outright and over the next fifteen years we were blessed with nine grandchildren, five girls and four boys. I also had the good fortune to be able to retire at fifty-four enabling me to support and devote time to our children and help raise the grandchildren. The house was transformed to accommodate six large bedrooms, three bathrooms, two kitchens and many playrooms for the children. In landscaping the grounds I planted fruit trees along the riverbank and along the different levels of the grounds unwittingly creating a restaurant for fallow deer and other wild life. I added slides, swings and ropes from trees for the children to play on. Over the year's, successions of our grandchildren's joyous laughter, was music to my soul as they played hide and seek in the orchard. What a better place for children to spend a warm sunny day than just messing about on the river. From a peaceful sandy ledge at the river's edge they spend happy hours fishing. The winter snow brought forth hoots of joy as they expended time and energy tobogganing down the steep banks either side of the orchard and skating on large ice formed patches.

For a long time family life was idyllic in our dream home with an enviably lifestyle, and a contented healthy family cocooned and enviably self-supporting. Until... Late one summer evening idly watching the news, I catch the word "Artane". That word sent a bolt of fear and dread right through my brain. The newscaster's voice continued as I forced my mind to focus on his words: "The Catholic Orders of the Christian Brothers in Ireland have taken up a full-page spread in a national newspaper to apologies for the abuses inflicted on children placed in their care years ago". The institution no longer existed. I'm in shock and inexplicably shaking and sobbing uncontrollably.

A concerned Jean rushes to my side. "What's wrong?" It takes me some time to respond as I rock to and fro like I did as a child in an Industrial School, only then without crying. "How dare they offer an apology for what they did to us children? Its fifty years too late". I didn't wish to see or hear anymore and sobbing I plead: "Please turn it off, turn it off".

I wonder will it be possible to put the genie back in the bottle and blank out the past a second time? No. Finally they have admitted it was real. Artane that accursed place did exist. Now I must face reality and come to terms and accept my stolen childhood. There's so many questions, yet so few answers. Why the admission now? I am over sixty years of age. Do I really want to know why a State Authority would take a babe in arms into custody? Then lock it away until the age of sixteen before setting it free to somehow survive in an alien world. But I do learn a lifetime later and the evidence defies belief.

For decades I had believed my demons were safely locked away in the darkest recesses of the mind. If just a hint, sight, sound or smell of those dark years surfaced I could expertly competently erase it in the blink of an eye.

But now in order to stay sane I must retrace my childhood journey down the torturous road of the past, to confront my demons and savour the blessings, and just maybe discover some answers.

Sadly after twenty-five glorious years living in our paradise I am left with the painful challenge of having to walk away from it all. The grandchildren's springtime is past. They have entered the summer of their lives with offspring's of their own.

Now I must devote the winter of my years to care for a very special baby, Jean, who was always there for me. Her love was always unconditional and inspirational. Alas she is stricken with the dreaded cruel illness of Alzheimer's. Like the faithful stray she took on all those years ago I chose to perform this labour of love on my own, defying the experts who say it's impossible.

CHAPTER TWO

A Child Called Charlie

I must have woken up. How did I get here? I know not who I am nor from whence I came. I sit in my cot rocking to and fro staring at the black shiny stove. The coals are burning red in the grate. On the top of the stove rests a flat iron, and when a hand reaches out and places a wad of cloth on the handle, it's grasped my full attention. The iron is lifted and splashed with water that hisses as it sizzles and bounces off its hot surface. I watch intensely as the hand places the iron in a silver shoe containing metal spring-like laces that clip into recesses in the heel of the shoe. The iron is now gliding along smoothing out the material on the ironing board.

On completing the ironing the figure clad from head to toe places the iron to one side and removes the freshly ironed clothing from the room. I take this opportunity to climb from my cot. The ritual of heating the iron fired my imagination. I pick up three discarded metal bottle tops and place them on the stove, with a view to using them as irons! Footsteps on the polished wooden floor sent me scurrying back to my cot. With a degree of annoyance in the voice: "How did these get here?" As the bottle tops are brushed into the nearby coalscuttle. On turning around I see in addition to the hands the only other visible flesh to the body, the face, bright and shiny. The white concealing below the chin, the ears, upper forehead and chest is in contrast with the veil resting on the head draped down the shoulders, blends in with the rest of the Habit. The gleaming gold cross lying across the chest can't help but catch the eye.

"I wonder if there is hair on the head, and how can it be possible to hear? I can't see any ears".

My thoughts are interrupted,

"You must be Charlie; I'm Sister Clare, are you all right?"

That's who I become known as, a name I come to respond to. It sounds a nice name, Charlie. Although I fail to reply she carries on talking even though it is beyond my understanding. "Always remember when a nun's speak to you must address us as Sister". When the Sister leaves, I start to take in the detail around me. With my back to the stove, to my left there are windows, which floods the room with light on sunny days. The opposite side and other walls large holy pictures adorn the walls. At each side of the room there are some six beds, feet facing the centre of the room. A dark brown wooden covered commode and a side locker separate each. This is the Infirmary, where the sick children are cared for. It's my favourite place to be in the whole of St. Patrick's Industrial School. It's run by the Sisters of Charity for male infants up to the age of ten, committed here by the courts for being orphaned, destitute, abandoned or charged with an offence under the then existing British laws of 1908 and 1924 acts. Many a contented hour I spent asleep here, when ill with a cold, to have my chest and throat painted with iodine and covered with cotton wool. My numerous boils were treated with a hot bread poultice to draw the puss to the surface and then squeezed out. In addition I was fed special food for my condition, a stew of potatoes, carrots, and other vegetables, which I wolfed down, a nice change from the daily "stir- about" (gruel). As an up patient I roamed freely around the infirmary. Most days I was content to play in the Veranda located on the same level as the bedroom, high up in the building. With its glass roof and surrounds it was airy and bright and allowed for beautiful views across a green landscape. The free-range hens having a dust bath on warm sunny days intrigued me.

The scent of new mown hay and the perfume of flowers wafted up on a gentle summer's breeze through open windows from the garden below on the opposite side. On the ground floor I came across an opening leading to a small courtyard. It was surrounded by a high hedgerow in which rested a beautiful bright-eyed robin. Like the one in the holy picture picking the thorns from Jesus head. As it flitted from branch to branch singing softly, at intervals I tried communicating by making similar sounds through my teeth and lips. It appeared to answer but when I slowly raised my hand in the hope of it coming to me, off it flew. It was always good to be back in the infirmary, once when I was visited with mumps, later with an ear infection, finally a serious illness. Feeling very tired, weak, and in pain from the lumps under each arm and the top of my thighs. So tired and weak I just wanted to sleep. I lay against a tree and remember nothing else, except waking up in a darkened room. My throat was sore; a glint of light shone through partly opened drapes.

A man and nun leaned over me. "Do you think you could eat some toast?" The nun enquired.

I do not wish to answer, as I wanted to stay ill, but hunger got the better of me. I nod to indicate yes. The doctor assures the nun: "He's going to be fine."

When next I wake I've been transferred to the infirmary. To this day the sight of that lovely cool glass of milk on the locker in front of my eyes haunts me.

"Oh how I wish I to quench my desperate thirst with that cool white liquid."

Sheer fear stopped me from touching it, I drift off to sleep, and when I awake it is gone. Soon I am fit enough I am moved on to the nursery. The infirmary is where I want to stay and will try to go back there. On a late autumn day I stand on the low wall in the playground whilst holding the railings I breath in deeply the smoke from the farmer's bonfire in the adjacent field, intending to become ill. Vaccination time results in a batch of us being taken to the infirmary. A silver cylindrical implement is placed on the upper arm. The doctor turns the other end making four separate circular cuts. Holding a thin short tube to his lips he blows a substance into each cut. The itching wound is taped with a dressing to protect it from scratching and infection. When the scabs are gone, the boys display four neat scars with pride. I was not so lucky, even after a second Vaccination, I'm left with no visible badge of pride on either arm. The visit of the dentist brought word, to have a tooth extracted meant receiving a sweet. That I wasn't going to miss out on, so I blackened one of my teeth, needless to say I failed in my ploy. On rare occasions visitors passing the playground threw sweets over the railings. This resulted in what we called a *Grush* i.e. a scramble, a test of the survival of the fittest.

It was whilst attending my first day in class I was to discover two new things about myself. Sister Germane address us: "Children I want you all to pay close attention to what I have to say, do you understand?"

"Yes Sister" we responded.

"Now who can tell me why you are here to day?"

Our hands shot up keen to answer. "Rice, put your hand down, now put up your other hand, and remember to use the correct hand in future".

I have come to dislike being called Rice, it's a warning that trouble is brewing. As no one responded with the correct answer, we were informed:

"You are now five years olds and ready to start your schooling".

The memory of that first day behind a desk would stay with me for the rest of my life. We are instructed to copy the words the Sister wrote on the blackboard. Taking my slate pencil in my left hand I proceeded to write on my slate. I hear my name: "Rice why are you using the wrong hand to write?" How can I reply? "I don't know Sister" Confused, I'm unaware there's a right and a wrong hand. Ordered out to the front of the class: "Hold out your hand" Not surprising I proffer my left. With a look of fury the Sister spits out. "That's twice you defied me, you still hold out the wrong hand, well this might teach you which hand to use in future".

Down comes the cane a number of times swinging and switching with gusto to achieve her objective by leaving the offending hand too sore to use.

As I notice the other children using their right hand to write, I'm different; there must be something wrong with me! Learning does not come easy in spite of trying hard to remember what I am told. I'm to be caned mercilessly for being impertinent by putting my wrong hand up in response to questions. That was until I discover a way of avoiding the beatings. I had a wart on my right palm near the wrist; thus I was able to sneak a look at my hands under the desk before deciding which hand to raise.

A pleasant and welcome change was the issue of new slates, ones with a wooden frame. They were lighter and easier to collect at the end of class.

In the two years leading up to the "Age of Reason" I acquired the ability to remember most of what I am told. There's the Ten Commandants and the Seven Deadly Sins, numerous prayers in English, Latin and Irish.

I'm not capable of giving much though to what I am saying.

After all how could I honour my father and mother as the Commandant says, "Who might they be?" It all sounds very nice, except for Adam and Eve. When one of them stole an apple from the garden and gave it to the other, who in turn took a bite, they were thrown out of the Garden of Eden. Because of them I started life with Original Sin, and now I must forever pray to be forgiven. I learn to sing and speak Latin at mass, I haven't the faintest idea what its all about, but it sounds important and nice. These words and saying I can still recall and repeat parrot fashion and yet they still remain meaningless, lodged forever in my brain. Told on reaching age seven we have achieved the Age of Reason and now are responsible for all our actions. With a number of other children it's time to make our First Communion. I jump with excitement thus creaking my neck. I take no heed of the pain for I'm so happy. We are taken into the playroom, and there in front of each of us lie a small pile of new cloths and the sweet smell of leather from shiny new boots.

I look forward to sitting at a special table in the refectory with the other boys for our first communion meal.

We will receive beautiful warm crisp soda bread, with creamery butter melting between the two halves. The smell of it make makes my mouth water. In the chapel everything is fresh and clean the smell of incense mixed with wax floor polish epitomizes the motto of the Sisters; "Cleanliness is next to Godliness'". Heads bowed, hands together in front of our face we each make our way forward, genuflect, kneel, heads tilted back and tongues out to receive the "Body of Christ".

From now on we must account for all our own actions by confessing our sins to a priest in the confessional. To be immodest is a sin, it means you must not show your body by taking your cloths off, without covering yourself. That's why we wear nightshirts that reach to the ankles. One night I was feeling adventurous. Because it was dark in the dormitory I think " God can't see me" so I got out of bed, lifted my nightshirt up to my waist, and quickly jumped back into bed. I had committed an "immodest"! It felt so very good to commit a sin. The down side, I would have to confess the sin at my next confession. It did help to make up the sin numbers though. I'm never sure about the immodest sin. For example when we are in the sewing room having our trousers repaired, being naked to the waist we are made to face the wall. But the nuns could see our bums! Surely that can't be right are we sinning? Then there was always the Old Faithful sin "using the wrong hand". Some of the Ten Commandments are easy to understand, like "though shall not steal". Others don't make sense: "do not covet thy neighbour's Wife", or "do not commit adultery".

What are they all about? I might be committing these sins unknowingly.

At best it's less sins to confess. Then there are the seven Deadly Sins two of these I understand, Pride, I am not sure I ever have anything to be proud of. As for Gluttony, I can't commit on that, there is never enough to eat, or otherwise I just might not mind having an ago at that one!

Hunger seems to stalk all of our daily lives, I think the sisters must be poor, as there never seems to be enough food. Having watched the other children I learned to subsidise my diet. Most days we spent a considerable time "up the field". This is a play field opposite the playground. There's a pathway up the centre, which leads to an open shed where the nuns sit, and pray, it also serves to shelter us from showers. To the right of our play field there are always rotating crops planted. While the nun is deep in prayer one of us would slip through the fence to retrieve heads of wheat, barley or corn, as others would keep *nicks* (lookout). Other years it would be mangles or turnips to feast on. The barren years to us were when the field was left as meadow or planted with potatoes. The whole convent grounds are set in farmland, in the field to our left cattle and horses grazed, the pathway between the playground and the fields' chickens freely roamed. In spite of there being seesaws, swings and slides, most of us search for food. This comes in the form of clover, clover flowers, dandelion leaves, sour leaves, the flower of the chestnut tree, the haws, and leaves of the hawthorn, these we call bread and cheese. There is also the rich red itchy back (rosehip) so called because the seeds placed down the back made one itch. Its red skin is crunchy, sweet and juicy. The shiny leaves from one tree, I now know to be the Silver Birch are plentiful, but the leaf I like best is a brown coloured one we know as the chocolate leaf. The clover flowers we know as honeysuckle, maybe because of the sweetness we find at the base when pinched from the flower head.

Some thirty years later whilst out running, along a country road I was stunned by the most fantastic aroma to assail my nostrils. I stopped to find from whence it came, but was unable. On arriving home I rushed my wife into the car, I just had to share this beauty with her. Imagine my surprise when my wife pointed out a creeping flower in the hedgerow saying:

"That's just honeysuckle!" Later she recounted the incident to a friend remarking, "He does strange things."

We made our own games; plucking the grass and pushing it up our jerseys as we moved on all four aping cows. There was also the horse and rider, one boy on all four with a piece of string in his mouth with a boy on top. One child's foraging for food proved to be fatal when he ate the pea like pods hanging from low lying branches of a yellow flowering tree, which I was to discover in the 1970's the tree's name to be the Laburnum. As a result the Reverend Mother gathered us around to warn us in the strongest terms of the dangers involved with the yellow flowering tree. A boy was now dead from eating the poisonous pods that hung enticingly like peas from its branches. The news of his death left me feeling without shock, sadness or fear. I knew of the boy but can't recall his name, but then I was different so kept much to myself. Rarely did I speak or played with the other boys.

My overpowering feeling for the dead boy was that of envy, though I knew it to be a sin. I could not deny it; after all he was going to meet *'Our Father, His Son and The Holy Ghost'* in heaven and be happy forever and ever.

I could vision him having great fun playing hide and seek with the *Holy Ghost* in and out of the clouds, not like the *Guy Guy* the scary ghost who lived down the bleach. That's where the nuns hang out the sheets and other washing on the lines which blow wildly in the wind and gives off a strong whiff of soap and bleach. Children, and nuns when they grow too old are buried in the graveyard nearby.

We were taken to see the dead child, laid out on a bed; he looked so peaceful like a beautiful Angel with pretty rosary beads entwined in the fingers of joined hands on his chest. As we kneeled beside the bed we prayed for his soul. He is in a peaceful sleep, except he had not got his hands crossed on his chest like we're supposed to do when we go to sleep. The funeral service was beautiful with lots of flowers and a wonderful gleaming white coffin. "Why do I sin by wanting what he now has?"

I never felt I could trust any of the other children, because one betrayed me by lying. We were playing in the communal lavatory *making sick* like we did, by stamping on the urine soaked red tiled floor in the centre of toilet. One boy relieved himself on the floor when no one was looking. We all rushed out screaming which caught the attention of a nun. Standing in a semicircle at lessons the Sister asked who had committed the foul deed.

A hand went up pointing at me, when asked if he was sure? He replied, "Yes". Called forward, protesting my innocence, but to no avail.

I was given a good trashing with the cane. It left me with a burning frustration which bubbled deep inside at the Injustice of it all I have never forgotten, and often wonder could that have been the seed which grew within me that still ignites anger within at the sight of any injustice to the vulnerable.

The food is nice enough only there never seems to be enough. There are lots of rice puddings, gruel, fried bread, bread and butter, and some times toast. We have two purposes to sneak a round of bread out of the refectory. One to take it into the playroom and rub it up and down on the large warm central heating pipes to "make toast". Of course it's no longer white but a little black, harder and warmer to convince us it's toast. The other use was to spit on bits of bread and stick them on the out side of the low wall below the fenced railings, boarding the playground. The chickens that roamed freely along the outside pathway would jump up to peck the bread. The game was to be fast enough putting ones hand through the railings and pet the bird. I had to confess my sin of stealing pieces of carbolic soap, after washing prior to bedtime. I'd acquired a liking for the taste. As I rarely play with any of the other children I make my own imaginary animal friends. I spent many an hour observing the farmer in the field opposite our playground with his plough and horses, turning over the shinny brown soil in straight furrows. In turn I would proceed to copy all his actions by ploughing in the playground. The most gratifying part was removing the harness from the horses for a well-earned rest and a long cool drink. At night time I'd keep them under my bed with the chickens, cows and Rover the Collie dog who worked on the farm. I'd go through imaginary tasks of feeding and cleaning them before giving each of them a 'good night' hug." Mrs. O'Shea with her greying hair in a tight bun at the back of her head sits knitting by a dimmed light 'till we all drift off to sleep. Often I watched the other children play games like *jackstones,* spinning tops or *foxes and hounds.* I once join in a Hurley knock about. All the other boys had proper Hurley sticks; mine was shorter as the handle was broken off.

In a melee for the ball I received a crack on the head that resulted in profuse bleeding. The duty nun took me into the nursery to clean the wound, which required a number of stitches. The doctor working on the wound remarked; "you're a brave boy not to cry."

I thought, it's a strange thing to say, did he not know boys don't cry. We're not supposed to cry we are always told, "boys don't cry", anyway what's to cry about? With the doctor's work finished the sister tries to apply a bandage around my head. I'm adamant I do not want it in spite of her threats:

"If you keep behaving like a baby I will put you in the nursery with the babies for the rest of the afternoon".

Just how can I explain, "Grown-ups don't understand".

Not wanting the other children to call me "scabby head". It had been drilled in to us "Cleanliness is next to Godliness", and so I preferred to spend the afternoon among rows of crying babies in their cots as they rock to and fro and side to side, as we all did from time to time. Who said rock and roll started in the fifties? We were doing it in the thirties! I didn't mind cleaning the excrement from the dirty nappies that are loaded in white enamel pales with blue-rimmed tops.

The freezing cold water, and the incessant crying of the children, bothered me more than the soiled nappies, as there appeared no end to it. I learn more by observing than being told everything. I'm fascinated watching workmen as they built a stonewall using shuttering held together with thick dowels on either side. Cement is poured between the boards along with rocks, left to set overnight, the dowels and shuttering removed and the holes left by the dowels cemented in. The resultant wall will last for many years to come. So clear was this visual instruction, I would come to build such walls thirty years later. As I observe the farmers move the haycocks from the fields on to the long flat bogies. Releasing the clip to let the metal covered end of the platform rest on the earth, this also released the wound up rope to be placed around the haycock. By ratcheting the handle at the front end of the bogy, the cogs mesh together, resulting in the haycock and bogy snapping upright once the hay had settled on the platform.

When the farmer has turned the soil with his plough to reveal potatoes, faceless women in bonnets and long shabby dresses appear as if by magic. They toil long hours collecting the spuds in the sacking around their waist.

In the summer time we help to air our mattress and make them more comfortable by teasing the fillings of flock or horsehair. Constantly moved around as though in a trance. By some unknown instinct we gather around in a pack, whenever a child was being given as 'Good Trashing' and join in the long waling of "Ah Law, Ah Law". The haunting sound that comes from the depths of the children's souls grow louder and mournful the longer the beating goes on. The sad sound comes easy and natural to be caught up in it, just as kicking out, growling and barking when being beaten around the body. It's a way of saying 'it's not fair'. Of course this kind of response only tended to infuriate the nuns which resulted in some doubling of efforts.

At last my time has come, I'm too old to stay, I must leave the convent. I'm dressed in all new cloths and boots, and am addressed by the Reverent Mother. "Well young man, you are all grown now you're ten years old, and its time to leave us, and move on to the Christian Brothers. You're such a dreamer, but I suspect you will make us proud of you and one day, and return to visit us wearing a nice gold watch and chain".

I've had the gold watch for many years now, times have moved on and watches on chains in vests are no longer. I'm not so sure now I'd like to fulfill the prophecy of a visit to St. Patrick's. I'm aware the nuns, God bless them did their very best by me. They could ill afford to become emotionally involved with so many children.

Now it's time to take my second journey as a lone young man, from Kilkenny Up to the outskirts of Dublin City (the city of my birth) to attend an Industrial School, the name of which would strikes fear in my heart at the very mention of it's name 'Artane'. It would be more than sixty years before I would learn that it ranked high in the world of Institutions for abuse against children in their custody.

CHAPTER THREE

Little Mister Nobody

Some protective instinct allowed me to consign certain memories to the deepest corridors of my mind. When called upon they refuse to surface.

Two such memories are the journeys and method of travel to St. Patrick's in County Kilkenny, and from there to Artane Industrial School, on the outskirts Dublin City.

Like most institutions of its kind and time they, were situated in remote countryside. Out of sight, out of mind. The main entrance to the school was a large wooden gate with high walls on either side. Inside there was a gatekeeper's lodge to the right. A long winding road bordered on either side by open fields' lead to buildings on the right, which housed the Christian Brothers. Confronting me at the end of the road were large high secure iron gates. At either side were equally high security railings. To my right there was a small narrow side entrance butted against a church wall. I was escorted through the small gate on to a large empty parade ground. My escort was a Christian Brother. We made our way along by the railing, passing the main gate, into a building. Up stairs I was ushered into the largest dormitory I've ever seen. There must have been hundreds of beds in long rows, each with a black metal tag at its head inscribed with bold white numbers. Now I was in the custody of the Christian Brothers. Like the nuns they are dressed head to toe in one colour, and wore a narrower dog collar than a priest's.

"I wondered why nuns are called Sisters and these men are called Brothers?"

My induction took the form of being told to strip naked. All my prized worldly possessions, the lovely new cloths and footwear given to me by the nuns, were confiscated. I would never see them again. A piece of paper containing two numbers was trust into my hand. "Get to know these numbers, number seventy-two (72) is your bed number over there". The Brother pointed to a bed half way up a middle row. "The other number you must remember for as long as you are at Artane, which will be for the next six years". What neither of us could have then know was I would remember the number eleven thousand, five hundred, and thirty-six (11,536) for the rest of my life.

I proceed to dress in the clothes laid on the bed, a collarless patched shirt I pull over my head and buttoned to the neck. There was a rough patched pair of shorts with suspenders to hold them up. The roughly darned socks at the heel reach my knees. A vest to button up over my shirt, a pair of heavy hob nailed boots with leather tong laces, the outfit completed with a coat containing a number of patches. They were so ill fitting it appeared as though I had stolen them from a scarecrow.

Soon I find myself to be just one more in a sea of other boys on the parade ground. Not only have I been stripped of my belongings, but also of my innermost feelings. My mind's shutters slammed down, only darkness existed. Escaping to my imaginary world had ended. Now I only wished to vanish as I recalled a poem from my last school, *"Mister Nobody"*. He was the invisible boy who left doors ajar, and rooms untidy. If this is where young men end up, then I found it frightening. I wished to melt away like *Mister Nobody* among all these other young men in this cold, fearful strange place. There were so many of them, different sizes and shapes.

Quickly I learned the daily routine by tagging along with the smallest and latest intake, most that arrived were from orphanages. I tagged along after them like a stray puppy. There was Joey

Brown, Charlie McGregor and Timmy O'Neil. Following them I learnt the ropes how to survive this "God fearing" place. On my first day I picked up on how to react at the blast of a whistle, there are commands to stand still, proceed, to sit, to eat, start or stop talking, or fall into our divisions on parade. Failure to react resulted in a beating and being placed on a charge. Charges were read out every Friday and offenders assigned guard duties, such as patrolling areas around the parade ground to ensure no one leaves the area without permission.

The opposite end of the Parade Ground to the main gate, the whole length is taken up with handball allies, except for doors at either end. To the left there was a large secure sliding door. Behind it the field we were released into in dry weather. The door to the right of the allies led to the Assembly Hall where we were herded when it rained. It was also used to keep the *"Nobodies"* (children without visitors) separate from the other children whose parents came on monthly visits with food parcels. In addition the *"Nobodies"*, a sum total of about thirty of us, from a total of approximately eight hundred, could watch the proceedings from inside the Hall. The children's parents' thronged through the now unlocked main gate. They also came to take their charges home for the duration of the Christmas, Easter and summer holidays, plus for the odd weekend. When the last of the parents had gone on holidays with their children the main gate was locked once again. We *Nobodies* had the whole place to ourselves for the duration of the holidays.

At the rear of the handball allies a pathway, lined a wall that was used as a latrine. We passed through there quietly from the dormitories every morning in single file to attend church. At night we made the return journey through the latrines to the dormitories. At first the stench of urine and excrement I found overpowering, I felt sick. One side was taken up by a flaking black painted wall were we stepped up to urinate, which then flowed into an open gully. The opposite side consisted of a row of toilet huts, each containing a half door. Inside each hut there was a wooden step with which to reach the seat and underneath there was a bucket. There was no toilet paper, resulting in the walls and surrounds of seats being used as an area to decorate with fingered marks of excrement. In time I failed to notice how soiled and wretched I'd become. If *"Cleanliness is next to Godliness* "what was this? Each time I passed through the latrines I was frustrated and confused. It appears I had no sense of direction. Everything around me appeared to have moved to opposite sides' overnight. It wouldn't be 'till much later in life the reasoning for my problem would become apparent, even my sense of direction would never improve. I had been born left-handed!

On our way to bed, emerging from the latrines, a large fresh water-drinking trough resting on a concrete plinth confronted us. It ran parallel with the wall, which lead to the dormitory door. The trough stood forward of the wall leaving a passageway of about three feet. Hangings by chains from the trough were about twenty cast iron goblets. Affixed long the broad length of pipe above the trough were about twenty whites tipped brass press-top cold water taps. Each morning we emerged from the dormitory's doors and marched in single file between the drinking trough and the wall, on through the latrines. Arriving by the Assembly Hall we took a right turn past the senior classroom window, where general information notices are displayed.

Taking a left at the corner of the classroom, situated to the left were the remaining classrooms.

At the farthest end of the row the junior classroom was located. This wide concrete area fronting the classrooms was used to line us up in our divisions, prior to being marched to our respective classrooms, or to the refectory. A blast of the whistle sent us dashing to form up facing the classrooms. There were twenty divisions each consisted of forty youths. These were further split into two, senior and junior. Divisions were graded by age; thus allowing the seniors first into the warmth of the buildings. At the next command we marched to our classrooms, the refectory, work or other activities depending on the time of day. The football pitch opposite the classrooms was cordoned off on three sides by concrete bollards; each connected by an iron bar. This area was out of bounds to all, except during summer holidays when the *nobodies* had the free run of it, to play Gaelic Football or Hurling. The railings set in a low wall attached to the church wall divided the pitch from the parade ground. There was however two bollards joined by a rail at the edge of the parade, at the opposite end to the church. These I came to witness were used to punish *"Runaways"* by forcing them to jump forward and back over while holding the bar.

They were encouraged in their endeavours with regular whacks of the strap, until they could no longer stand. Looking across the Parade Ground and past the football pitch stood the long refectory building. High in the front of the building was the clock tower, the clock that governed our daily lives. It was imperative I learnt to tell the time if I was to avoid additional punishment. At first I found it difficult, but over a period I discovered by counting in fives, tens, fifteen twenty etc. I mastered the secret of reading the clock, achieving a small glimmer of success. Each day as the clock hands moved towards mid day, the church bell rang signalling us to form up for the Angelus recital. We were all on tender hooks as we await the next blast from Brother Kiely's whistle. At the command we quickly formed singles files either side of a long baker's tray, which rested on trestles. Lunchtime for the under fourteens, the trays were laden with half slices of buttered black bread. We marched orderly to the tray and took our half slice. Ruling through fear, Kiely maintained a tight control over us.

We knew to always give him a very wide berth. A tall man of broad statue, with dark thinning hair, a long thin face with pointed nose.

Should one of us be unfortunate enough to catch his strong cent of tobacco and the musty smell of snuff, it's too late, we'll already have felt the sharp sting of his strap on some part of our body. Kiely had no need to speak, like a sheepdog he had complete and perfect control of all his flock.

As he approached we scatter like sheep.

The afternoon of my first day I was joined by the other boys and introduced to the daily forced run around the parade ground. The unaccustomed heavy hobnailed boots and darned socks blistered my heels, and the rough trousers chaffed my inner thighs adding to my discomfort. It is an uneven race with most of those nearing fulltime work age at the front of the field whilst beginners like me lagged behind. I watched the older youths slow down as they reached the drinking trough. Then they made a mad dash for the narrow gap between the trough and the wall, where Brother Comeford was strategically placed, to enjoy the game of out witting us. My legs were a little unsteady, but my survival instinct propelled me through that narrow gap avoiding the flawing strap. He always managed to mark some of us with more than one red welt.

It came as a great relief to stop and hobble towards the Brothers who beckoned me aside. One of whom produced a tuning fork, which he pinged and put to my ear, I'm instructed to sing, "Doe, Ray, Me". From the result of the test I'm informed: "You'll be joining the choir or maybe the band." It's good to be chosen for the band, it meant special treatment. Band members live in a different world, they travel and play at events all around the country. I'm then unaware they're used as a showpiece, to extol the virtues and achievements of the school. After a short period of attending band classes it became apparent I'm incapable of being 'taught' music. I can still recall being told, to remember, EGBDF, FACE, above and below the stave, quavers and semi quavers. Like Latin, I still haven't the remotest idea what they were trying to convey. My failure resulted in being assigned to work each day in the machine room. The machine room was a hive of activity, there were sowing and knitting machines laid out around the workshop. From now on 'till I'm fourteen, I make and repair shirts, finish off the toe ends of socks using four knitting needles to cast off stitches to complete the sock. I repaired coats, shirts, trousers with patches and darn holes in socks and jerseys, useful skills for a young man of ten. Working there was to my liking, learning all the jobs with the exception of using the knitting machines. Rarely did I need to answer any questions. I came to fear questions; knowing getting them wrong resulted in punishment. Because of my inability to furnish the correct answers in class I came to accept daily beatings as a normal part of life. In time I learnt to compete with other workers in making a complete shirt from start to finish without breaking the cotton. I received some *"hippers"* (slang for strap on the hand) when I broke a needle in the rush to be first. My first day in class set the tone for all future methods the Brothers employed in my education.

I sat engrossed trying to do joined up writing, known as the Creamer System. Using a pen nib at the tip of a wooden handle I dip into the inkwell to start writing on graph paper, with blotting paper ready to soak up any blots. The graph paper helped to ensure uniformity of letters and space. Suddenly I was lifted off my seat from behind by hands grasping at my locks. I let out a yelp more in anger than hurt that I spit out the word "Pig!" at the Brother. I'm towed to the front of the class by the ear. In spite of hearing what I had said, he asks: "What did you call me?" Defiantly and loudly I reply. "You heard, Pig!."

His dark eyes glowed furiously with rage. His face a picture of sheer disbelief. In his fury he beats me about the body with his strap, his voice came tight and hard:

"What do you have to say now?"

Gritting my teeth, "Pig!" I growl. The beating continues until I could no longer persist in the unequal match. With my tail between my legs I surrendered and grudgingly give him what he wished to hear. "I'm sorry" I learnt never be so stupid as to engage in such an unequal battle with any Christian Brother again.

The next memorable beating in class was some years later. It was during English spelling lessons. I'm unaware how English is taught at schools in the outside world.

Here the order came. "Spellings, open your books, and page one to twenty-five". For the next fifteen to twenty minuets the hurried fearful chattering of voices spelling different words from those pages can be heard. Over the noise came the dreaded words, from the *teacher*.

"Times up close your books". Starting with the front row, *teacher* picks a word. The boy next in line and the ones further along are praying hard they will be lucky in this lottery. The losers fall out to the side of the class; I was always one of those. The test over, we losers are lined up to accept our punishment; we each receive a number of *"hippers"*. On a memorable occasion for me, there were two boys lined up before of me. While laying into the first one, the sound of coins spilling to the floor unleashed a frenzied scramble, the strap had split open and coins were strewn all over the floor! As the precious coins are being snapped up, the class was totally out of control, bodies pushing and falling as they fought over the coins. The strap became ineffective. To restore control the Brother grabbed the wooden pointer and lashed out in all directions resulting in the narrow end snapping. Turning it around he used the thicker end to better effect in regaining control. It was my misfortune to be in his line of fire as I felt its force crack on my lower right shin. For the next weeks I was left with a limp. The swollen wound had to be lanced leaving a scar, clearly visible to this day.

Classroom violence against the 'students' was normal practice and in one case it got out of hand. The boy involved was Liam Fagan. Liam was seen "heading a ball" in the parade ground. The Brothers construed this as an insult to national pride. To head a ball whilst playing rushie (a kick about) with a tennis or rag ball, was considered to be indulging in the evil English foreign game of Soccer and grossly disrespectful to the country. Two classes were conducted back to back to back in each schoolroom. Our class was disturbed by a commotion from the class to our rear. Someone was receiving an almighty beating. Our teacher Brother Casey rushed to the other class. As we turned to watch their teacher kneeling over Liam, in a fit of rage holding him by the neck whilst banging his head against the floor. Casey pulled his fellow Brother off and ushered him to the Assembly Hall to calm him down. Liam is a *Nobody* who will not cry, but for some reason unknown his face fails to display any emotion. This type of reaction or lack of it only further enrages the brothers, but for us it brings a flicker of joy to our hearts knowing we're one up on them. With the exception of a Mr. Corrigan who we knew as "*Soaker*", the teachers were all Christian Brothers.

His method of getting his message through to student was to threateningly sit on a desk in front of his pupil, one foot resting on the seat, while he awaited a response to his question. Unsatisfactory answers resulted in the pupil receiving a punch in the nose causing a blood soaked face, hence the nickname.

All my praying brought little respite from the daily miserable suffering. In my first winter years I try to keep warm when outside on the parade ground, by huddling up against other small fellows leaning against a wall. The smell of unwashed bodies and stale urine wafted like steam from a cooking pot, sleeves were caked with snot, but together we gain some warmth. It always appeared my fate to be on the outside of the group studying the tiny crystal balls at the end of hair, and observing lice crawling on heads. To warm us while formed up on parade were ordered to bend at the waist and vigorously pump our arms across our bodies. The constant scratching between my fingers and toes brought little respite from itching only to make them wet and raw. At night I'm irritated by an itch to my bottom due to small white worms wriggling about.

Prayers were the order of the day before and after meals, before and after class, prior to bed and on arising, followed by Mass and of course thrice a day the angelus. I prayed outside these times, to get through the day without a beating, also that I am granted a large portion of bread at the evening meal. Mostly my prayers went unanswered. "Can this be what's meant when they say *suffer little children*? I understand the suffering, but why little? On this much food I won't grow very big". The one daily topic of conversation is raised by way of a question, "What are you on tonight?" This refers to the evening meal, when the loaf of black bread is cut between four.

Twenty boys are seated at each refectory table. Laid out on each table were twenty knives, enamel plate's, mugs, five loafs, and five small white enamel plates containing dripping that has set firm. We march in to stand by our bench, say grace before meals, followed by a whistle, the signal to sit, then the signal to eat, followed shortly by the signal to speak. The loaf, which measures about nine inches long by five, inches high. When it was my turn to be *last pick I* proceed to evenly cut the loaf into four. Then I sectioned the dripping into four equal parts. What's remained after the others had their pick is mine. Bread we referred to as *yang* and dripping as *monyum*. Other foods had nicknames to, such as, gravy was known as *slurry* and potato yachts, because of their often green and slimy appearance. The meal finished with, we use of our knifes to sweep up the crumbs onto our hand, and pop them into our mouths. This practice remained ingrained, so much so that in recent years I was made conscious of it when overhearing one of our grand children whisper, "Mom why does Granddad scoop up the crumbs?" "To understand you have to know what it's like to go hungry". Came the reply. Hunger was a constant companion; on occasions in desperation we would play *half'os* which meant we would agree to the loaf and dripping being divided in two. Two of us would agree to go without for the benefit of the others, the rolls being reversed at the next meal, hence the question "What are you on tonight?". The whole meal would end on the command of the whistle to cease talking, followed by the signal to stand and recite grace after meals.

For us who spent all our time locked away, the special foods we eagerly looked forward to each year were the two eggs we receive for Easter, two sausages for Christmas breakfast and most of all Christmas dinner. We would be ecstatic at what we were about to receive, repeating only the special contents of the meal to ourselves. Repeated as if it were but one joyous word *ham-roast-peas-pudding and wine.* This being the only time in the year we would taste such items. The pudding of course was Christmas, and the wine was a soft drink. The other great thrill was to receive real white bread for meals, delivered by an outside bakery, Johnson, Mooney & O'Brien, when all the other children had left on holidays. A special food to catch my imagination, leaving me with a longing to taste, was the sight of smooth red shiny tomatoes brought by a visiting parent for her offspring. Years after my discharge to the outside world; I came to discover the taste didn't remotely match my longing imagination.

The first winter seemed longer and colder than any other did. The craving hunger, the pain of chilblains, the irritation of lice and worms plus the punishments seemed never ending. As the weather changed I came to accept these minor irritants. Gradually I begin to integrate and engage more in games and conversation with the other boys. I take to playing handball in the allies, and

Jackstones with Charlie McGregor and Joey Brown. Playing a game of *three and in* with Charlie is both competitive and enjoyable. By laying our coats on the ground we mark out a goal, with one of us stood between the coats the other kicks the rag ball to try and score. Once three goals are scored the roles are reversed. The gap, which exists between the drink trough and wall, serves as a goal when we propel the ball with our hands. Sometimes the ball gets caught on a roof or gutter, this we refer to as *canting* the ball.

With Charlie's dare devil attitude he's sure to retrieve it, he loves climbing and is ever the risk taker, and lovable show off. The yarns the city kids tell of their exploits, scutting on the backs of lorries to get around the City, in addition to playing pitch and toss, and being regular corner boys captivated him. They proudly show off stories in the newspapers (brought by parents) highlighting their father's exploits which end up with them in prison. Some of their family members make headline news and that is something to boast about. Charlie's mischievous actions could cause others to land up in trouble. There's one occasion after a meal; I see a smirk on his face at grace after meals when he chooses to utter his own version.

"God be praised me belly is raised an inch above the table". This rendition is received by some of us with stifled giggles, resulting in us being punished. Joey Brown is the closest I ever came to accepting as a friend. He must be a little older than I must, because he started fulltime work before me. We had become aware that we were approaching age fourteen. It's by then we're moved up to the senior class to complete our *education,* after which we started full time work. Whatever Joey chose I was sure to follow in his footsteps. He looked out for me. In spite of us falling out, and failing to talk for long periods, come the summer holidays we would be thrown together when only the *nobodies had* the run of the school.

Either he or I would kick a ball towards the other, it would be returned. In that simple act, a conversation would ensue and past differences would be forgotten. During the holidays we were inseparable. At the start of my first summer holiday at Artane, when the parents arrived at the front gate to take their boys' home for holidays. There was a deep felt longing and shame at having no one coming for me. It summoned up the courage in me to tell the Brother in charge that my parents were coming to pick me up. Surprisingly he accepted my story (another sin) and allowed me on to the parade ground to join the other boys. I felt totally alone in spite of being in the presence of all these boys. I'd dared to wish the impossible, wishing and hoping is all I had left. My fists clenched by my side, I concentrated with every fibre of my being wishing and praying for a miracle. "Please let me have parents to take me home, and I promise to be good". After all, I have been told of countless miracles. Time seemed to move at a snails pace. I'm alone as the last kid leaves with his parents, as I hang on in hope, there's a heavy silence around the vacant ground. I feel eyes boring into the back of my head from the Assembly Hall. Slowly I make my way back to rejoin the rest as I swallow any shred of pride left, accept reality and stop trying to fool others and myself. Who was I trying to fool?

"I'm nobody why should anyone want me?".

Joey comes towards me with a look of relief:

"What happened?" Shrugging my shoulders:

"They were too busy to come"

I lie for the second time that day.

During these few school years I unconsciously adapt to the daily routine of the institution. In addition to work, school, attending church daily, the never-ending prayers, there's the daily drill and marching. A serving army soldier visits to instruct us in the latter. He's known as *drainer* because of the constantly hanging dewdrop on the end of his hooked nose. Supervising some of the boys' weekly showers is also part of his duties. Friday night is cloths changing night. Bundles of cloths are dumped in the Dormitory changing room. The survival of the fittest determined who grabbed the best of the clothing to leave the rest with the oldest the most patched and darned garments. Each Saturday, wearing the freshly laundered cloths we wound our way along snakelike, in pairs down backcountry lanes. During these walks we're on the look out for anything edible such as a discarded apple butt, blackberries, sloughs, haws or rosehips. Timmy and I keep *nicks* (lookout) from the Brother and monitor escorts, Charlie, the dare devil as ever would break ranks to retrieve the food. For our Sunday walks we wore our best set of cloths, ones without patches. These walks took us to the outskirts of the city passing shops where the aromas floating in the air left us with what can only be pictured as something we might only dream of tasting. The mix of smells, which emanated from the chemist's shop I always imagined, must be the same as a bunch of differing flowers. The only flowers, which could be seen in the school, were those displayed in the church.

There were occasions of entertainment, such as a fight between two of the older boys. We gather around the fighters straining to get a good view of the contest. From the back of the circle of spectators the Brothers show a keen interest. When things got out of hand the Brothers would wade in with straps flying. In situations such as these, Joey, Charlie, Timmy and I howl with laughter at the strange cries of "Mammy, Daddy" the kids' make when whipped with the strap. We found it strangely funny to hear young men calling for their parents and even crying, just because they are being beaten!

During the Christmas holiday, the long dark evenings were spent in festively decorated classrooms. We played board games such as Snakes and Ladders, checkers and one which we threw rubber rings at a board that contained numbers and hooks.

Timmy appeared to be constantly chewing. His habit of "chewing the cud" was irritating and revolting. In response to my expressed dislike of the habit he stuck out his tongue that contained regurgitated food, "See I can have my food twice". Offering, "Would you like some?".

In spite of this revolting habit I found him a very interesting and clever fellow. He'd made needles from a piece of wire removed from a fence. By flattening one end with a flat stone, then inserted the eye, by driving a hobnail extracted from his boot through the flattened end. The opposite end he sharpened on smooth stone. The needle we used to sew up rag balls for playing with. Whenever possible I managed to appropriate proper needles, cottons and patches from my workplace at the machine shop. The needles and cotton I left behind my lapel, the patches stuffed in my pocket, that I'd *forgotten* about after work! Timmy made a beautiful propeller from a piece of wood it was so smooth and well balanced. When he held it up to the wind on the end of a piece of wire it whirls around at speed. He was so inventive.

It must be have about half way through my school years when the preparation for my Confirmation commenced. Though unsure of its meaning, I was aware I'd have to visit an outside church dressed in my Sunday best for the ceremony. It also entailed choosing a second Christian name. Learning the Catechism was a prerequisite, which was done in parrot fashion, I had to remember it all in preparation for my oral examination by visiting priest.

Facing questions was always a time of great trial and fear. This was one test I tried to hide my nervous fear from the priest. Like a parrot I responded correctly to all question, until one stumps me.

"How is Mary related to Joseph?" Silence, bursting with fear, my mind was racing, I knew it was either husband or wife, which? Gently the priest asked, "Mary and Joseph, are they brother and sister", that's easy I thought. "No".

Asked again, I respond quickly, "Mary…." I drew out the answer to gain time to think with my heart pounding; this was a fifty-fifty question and so: "Mary is Joseph's husband" I blurted, the priest smiled. "You mean wife?" I lied, "Of course". Relief, I'd passed without being strapped.

Word got around that Brother Kiely had finished at the school, he must have been retiring. We wondered what the new Brother would be like, as he would assume the mantle of Lord and Master of the parade ground. At lunchtime a squat well-built man named Druidy appeared among us for the first time.

With ruddy face, curled lips displaying a set of piano shaped teeth he gave the impression of a permanent sneer or snarl. His head was crowned with thick red hair swept back in tight waves without a parting. It was midday; as usual the bread was laid out on the baker's tray. On the command of the whistle absolute pandemonium broke out. A mad scramble for the bread resulted in the tray being knocked over, fighting pushing, bodies falling all over, eager outreached hands grabbed for bread. I manage to get a squashed fistful of bread. These few moments of mad freedom were exhilarating. It took a while before Druidy, a younger and fitter man than his predecessor regained control of the mob. In time he also proved to be a tougher taskmaster. With the arrival of the warmer weather my chilblains faded, but are replaced by weeping sores about my body from my constant scratching of a non-stop itch. Treatment for this condition was to apply Jeyes' Fluid to the affected parts. In the Assembly Hall striped to the waist and in single file, we formed a moving circle around a tin bath perched on chairs. Dipping our hands into the black milky liquid we rubbed over our sore bodies, bringing relief from the itch. Any bare skin exposed to the sun however resulted in extremely painful burning. There was no preventing the back of my neck from being burnt.

Joey, being older than I, had chosen his trade, in full time work. A Poultry Farmer was a very wise choice, I soon learnt why. At the end of his day's work I rushed to meet him as he entered the side gate to the parade, his pockets full of goodies. Always there was white bread, leftovers from the Brother's dining room. Not surprisingly when it was my turn to choose a trade I'd already made up my mind like Joey I had to be a Poultry Farmer, if only for the food. Moving up to the senior class was a marker to indicate I must have been nearing fourteen and about to finish school. It also gave me an indication for the first time in my life of how old I was. Now it was time to start work at my chosen trade.

My final Saturday walk along deserted lanes would linger forever in my memory. Joey and Timmy had already started work; I was paired up with an unknown youngster. Charlie was further up the line and out of sight. A large truck moved slowly up behind us, shortly after passing us there's a big commotion up front. The truck has stopped, we all gather around. There to the left of the truck lay Charlie crushed on the ground. Pure animal curiosity got the better of me; blood trickled from the right side of his mouth and his left ear. His body lays limp like a rag doll. I felt nothing; I was unaware of the total emotionally barren half-dead feeling inside me. I had accepted this in my stride as part of life. He must have tried to copy what he learned from the city slickers, to experience the excitement of scutting on a truck. By jumping on the side instead of the back, his foot must have caught in the wheel. I banished the memory from my mind. It took a repeated incident years later to make my blood run cold as it triggered the memory back into sharp focus, to feel real pain, sorrow and all the other emotions which should have been there then. Charlie's coffin lay in the church for a day or so.

Some of us spent a little more time in church than we might normally have done during playtime. This was a new dark experience, seeing a dark brown wooden casket looking so forlorn and out of place. We used the church at playtime during very cold weather to escape the cold by pretending to pray. Many a time one or other of us were caught talking which resulted in a good and deserved beating. Charlie's funeral was notable by the absence of any man or women, no Mother or Father, no one to bid farewell, only a small number of selected boys. I give no thought as to why or who were chosen to be there, only aware of a number of Brothers and a priest. The ceremony conducted by the priest I failed to focus on. My mind wandered to the memory of the boy who lit up this God forsaken place with a beam of sunshine, by way of his irreverent devilish grin and wild antics. My thoughts were sharply interrupted hearing a Brother speaking of Charlie. His words spark anger within me. "Do my ears deceive me?" "Charlie was a little wild, but full of fun and mischief, a lovely boy non-the less".

These words spoken by a member of a *gang* who constantly tried to "beat the sunbeam of mischief out of him." In order to shut my mind to such hypocrisy I let it wander to another time and place.

I recalled him telling me how he watched two of the smaller boys playing funerals in the field, burying an insect in a matchbox. One was playing the Priest saying: "In the name of the Father, and of the Son and into the hole he goes." Maybe Charlie is laughing at me now, knowing he is free at last. After the funeral any credibility I may have had in the Brothers' teachings were badly damaged, and the flicker of light that was Charlie was snuffed out.

If at any time I felt I could not suffer any worse violence than I had experienced to date I was sadly mistaken. It is late into the night and I was soundly asleep. A hand roughly grasped at my nightshirt yanking me awake. A harsh voice whispered "Get up" I was dragged from my bed. The whole dormitory was sound asleep. By now I was wide-awake with fear when I recognise the dreaded Brother we call *Bocker*, who was dragging me into the changing room. His Co. Cork accent I had great difficulty in understanding him when speaking English, (let alone Irish), that he was using. He closed the door and ordered me to remove my shirt. A despairing depression settled over me, as I stood necked in front of him, shaking with fear. Using a strong dialect his voice was deep and husky: "What were you doing today?"

In a state of panic and fear I can't conjure up any misdeed I may have committed. "I don't know." Whack! I feel the leather cut into my shoulder. He continues. "What were you doing in the field with those other boys today"?

Now wide-awake; my brain was racing searching for an answer, in spite of not receiving a clue as to what he may be referring. "I was wrestling with them," I blurted. Crack, I felt the strap on my legs, I turned, I felt its sting across my back time and again. There was no let up, his voice now impatience:

"I ask you again what were you doing?"

No inspirational excuse came to me.

"What does he want me to say?"

I made up a lame answer:

"I kicked the other boy".

At this answer he flew into a rage and sets about beating me unmercifully as I curled up into a ball trying to protect as much of my body as possible. He kicks at me. "Get up". Panting he still awaits an answer. Desperately I search my mind for the worst sin I can commit. A fleeting thought:

"No one's dead, if only there was I could admit to killing, then the hurt would stop". Sweat glistens on his forehead as he carries on beating.

There's a break, summoning up all my strength I'd left I plead:

"Please I don't know anything". After another few swipes, he opened the door, and threw my shirt after me, and in a panting quiet harsh whispered:

"Get out of my sight". As I crawled out the door, agitated he spits out. "Get up!" I stumbled and hobbled to my bed and struggled under the sheets without bothering to put on my nightshirt. After a fitful night's sleep my bruised body was stiff with pain. My eyes felt ragged and had trouble keeping them open; already I was wishing the new day to come to an end.

Drainer our drill instructor was monitoring during our weekly shower. I heard the tone of alarm in his voice. "What..." I turned to see open-mouthed look of surprise on his face. "What in God's name happened to you?" Questions, fear surged through me, what do I say? I hated questions. With my head hung in shame as he looked at my bruised and battered body. "I fell down," I mutter.

As he moves slowly away I hear him, talking as if more to himself.

"If people on the outside only knew..." his voice tailed off.

Later that evening I spied "*Bocker*" on the Parade Square. I tried to make myself scarce not ever wishing to see his evil, black curly headed face again. Bad luck, he'd spotted me. With peppy strides he closed the distance between us. I felt like a rabbit caught in a car's headlights. He sidled up to me and in a voice just above a whisper tries to excuse his attack on me.

"Maybe I went a bit too far last night, but I hope you understand, it hurt me more than it hurt you!"

Not replying I shuffled away from him, he exudes an odour of pure evil. Feeling dirty I had nothing but hate and contempt toward him. He'd killed something within me. Black clouds of nothingness enveloped me, which allowed me to drift through each day as they melted into each other.

To date there had been only two escapees, and one released boy who were returned. Of the two, which we referred to as *runways* one got away, the other was caught and returned. It thrilled us no end to hear stories of "Gunny" Shay, he managed to avoid capture. He was a streetwise kid from

Dublin City a *bousie* (young thug); rumour had it he was in for stealing.

Others of his pals were in for *mitching"*(non-attendance at school) begging, mother in prison, or for "frequenting the company of a reputed thief or prostitute" to mention but a few crimes. From these boys we learned "*Gunny*" had dyed his hair red and kept changing addresses and spent a lot of his time in picture houses (Cinemas).

The second boy who tried to escape was also a *nobody*. He never stood a chance lacking knowledge of the outside world. In just a short few days he was found hiding under a hedgerow by a potato field. He was given the standard treatment for 'runaways' a *mooner* (his head shaved till shawn) to mark him out from everyone. He was to be shunned; anyone caught speaking to him would be punished. In addition he was compelled to go through the punishment of jumping to and fro over the barrier.

Another of the *nobodies* was returned. On completing his time at Artane he had been disposed of. (*The official term for being hired out*) The reasons for his return were displayed on the information board in the school window for everybody to read. It appears the people he'd been farmed out to, were unhappy with his work output. Each detailed misdemeanour made it appear as though he accepted his guilt in his own handwriting:

"I failed to get up on time, to chop the wood and light the fires in time for breakfast" etc. It was written as an admission of his failings in 'his own words'. His punishment was the same as that of a runway. How could I hold any respect for the Order of the Brothers? Now I wanted to be like the other lads. I learned swear expressions, such as: *feck off, your aulone and your oulfella* (oulone and oulfella refers to ones parents with disrespect). I was preparing myself for the outside world! Time to join Joey in fulltime work was nearer and when asked the choice of trade I wished to undertake there was only one, I'm going to feed myself every day from now on. One thing puzzled me, "Why did the Brothers receive more and better food than they can eat?" I reasoned they are already big, we were the ones who required building up.

Prior to my starting work I recall a newspaper cutting appeared on the information board. It announced that the Prime Minister had sent a letter of condolence to the German Embassy on the death of Hitler.

I believe the Brothers were sad on receipt of this news. Word got around that Jimmy Carney the senior and most respected of the *Nobodies* was due for release had told the senior Brother: "Once I'm outside I'll never attend church again."

I understand this shocked the Brothers but they were helpless to do anything about it. For his age Jimmy was big and strong enough to take on any one of them as an equal. I felt elated that after that after six years in their custody they had failed in their endeavours to brainwash Jimmy.

CHAPTER FOUR

Working My Keep

I'm overwhelmed with joy knowing at long last my final year of schooling was over. My last summer holiday had signalled the end of my days as a youth. From here on I was grown up and about to start working for my keep. It should also mean an end to the almost daily beatings due to the dreaded questions, daily drill and forced running. Initially there were no vacancies available on the poultry farm. Therefore I was temporary assigned to work on the farm. As it is late summer early autumn the trashing machine was to be my first workplace. A large burley ginger haired man grasped me by the shoulder. His course, collarless shirt with the sleeves rolled up to the elbow revealed a thick lightly downed hairy arm as he reached out to pull back a canvas covering. As he pushed me into a small dark enclosure:

"In you get to fill the bags with him". With the flap down my eyes adjusted to the dark surrounds. In the dim light I could make out the shape of a dust sprinkled shaven headed fellow cowering in the darkness as he held out a Hessian sack to collect the wheat chaff as it poured down a shoot. His eyes were sad and appeared devoid of hope. As my eyes adjusted to the light, I recognised him! He was the runway who was caught hiding in the hedgerows. I was moved by sadness, then anger at the sight in front of me. Overcome with compassion I felt compelled to strike up a conversation,

"My name's Charlie, what's yours?" Startled he cowered as he replies;

"Your not supposed to be talking to me." Of course I was only too well aware but with a show of bravo: "I know but I don't give a feck about any one anymore."

"Con's me name" he whispered "OK Con, what are we supposed to be doing here?"

He proceeds to show how the bags are filled, tied and left outside. As the work progressed he became more relaxed. We're chatting and laughing when suddenly the flap is raised flooding the place in light. I'm grasped by scruff of my coat collar and yanked out by the same arm that first pushed me in. Held up in his big fist like a curled up pup, dropped on his instep I let out a yelp as he boots me to the other side of the footpath. This being the extent of my punishment I consider I'm very fortunate on two counts. One the Brothers never get to learn I had broken a rule by speaking to a runaway. The other was being kicked in the only area of my body that cushioned the impact.

With work rotation I was glad to be reassigned work in the barnyard. Here I benefited by laying my hands on extra food, filling my pockets with ears of corn, wheat and barley when I'm out of sight of my overseer. I looked forward to enjoying the spoils on my return to the school grounds after work. My new boss is a tall wiry man with thick black hair, a face dark with stubble and soft brown eyes. I followed him up the ladder to the hayloft, carrying a pitchfork about three times my size. While we awaited the first loaded hay cart's arrival, he instructed me in the use of the pitchfork by pitching hay over our heads to the next empty level.

"We can't allow the hay to pile up, it would be unwise to upset the fellows below to let hay fall back down. We must keep up the pace, now you'll need to rest while we wait."

The rattle of metal covered wheels across the cobble stone yard combined with the smell of fresh horse droppings from below disturbed my fitful sleep. With the arrival of a loaded cart the men began pitching the hay up to our feet with a smooth easy and experienced action. In turn we pitched it over our heads. With every ounce of strength I could summon I tried to keep up the pace. By comparison my companion pitched with an easy economical movement, his arms lean and hard with muscles that stood out like thick strands of rope. From his efforts I caught an honest healthy odour of sweat. With my shirt damp, my arms and shoulders ached with my endeavours to please. At last the sound of the cart leaving brought a relieving break to the work. "Eh kid, for a little one you sure try hard enough, you've earned your rest between loads".

Bunching up my coat and vest into a pillow I laid down and drifted off to sleep. Soon I was pitching again, with his words of praise still ringing in my ears they served to wash away my aches and pains and urged me to greater efforts for the remainder of the workday. Although I ached in places I never knew existed, for a rare moment it felt good to be given a sense of self worth.

In addition there was yet the feast of my ill-gotten grain to enjoy.

It was now late autumn and the colder early mornings were getting darker. Once again work rotation found me performing a different aspect of farm work. A cold damp morning saw a group of us set out to work in the fields to gather and snag mangles. The work must have been back breaking for the two big farm hands who act as overseers. Intermittently they stood and stretched to ease their aching backs. By contrast a small urchin such as myself, found the dew-drenched vegetables make my fingers numb with the cold. We uprooted and relieved the mangles of their leaves with the use of a sharp knife. The damp, mud and seemingly endless rows yet to be tackled left me wishing for the day's end.

At last the news I'd being longing to hear, Joey informed me a vacancy on the poultry farm was imminent. Eagerly I looked forward to eating well once I began working my chosen trade. With the light fading on the fields it brought our workday to an early finish. Returning to the parade ground we played handball or rushie. The latter consisted of a football game using an old tennis or rag ball, keeping it down on the ground at all times. Raising to head it, was considered to be playing soccer, an English game that was strictly forbidden. One of the skills of the game was to shoulder your opponent off the ball. To counter the shoulder charge one ducked low at that precise moment to avoid contact, thus sending one's opponent over your back crashing to the ground. The most gifted player was a lad named "Mixer" Madden. Sadly "Mixer" never returned from his summer holidays with his parents, we heard he'd drowned. Left to our own devices we discover self defence and attack by using elbows, shoulders, knees, and fists in clinches, and use of legs to throw opponents. Unwritten rules forbade kicking, scratching, biting, or head butting. It was a matter of honour that fighting may only be conducted on a one on one basis.

To break these rules would bring forth the wrath of the others and result in a good hiding from a number of bigger fellows.

On an evening whilst playing we were distracted by a Brother as he strolled across the football pitch carrying a wire cage full of rats. They sure weren't from around our dining or living quarters for they looked too fat. A rough red haired terrier dog accompanied him. We didn't need encouragement to flock towards the railings and watch the spectacle of rats being released from the cage while the dog dashed to and fro catching, shaking and killing them. It was a very rare moment of entertainment and excitement in our mundane lives, obviously a show put on for our entertainment.

It's winter when I started work at my chosen trade. The change brought a newer and freer life style. The colder weather went unnoticed, as I was kept very active cleaning the dropping boards and perches in the hen houses. There are also the geese, ducks and turkey houses plus the hen houses to be cleaned out and bedded down with straw. Daily the livestock are watered and fed, plus eggs had to be collected, and nest boxes to be made up.

We used large heavy wooden wheelbarrows to transport bales of straw, plus the waste from the dropping boards and livestock's floors. My hands could just about span the thick handles of the barrow, and just about manage to lift a loaded barrow off the ground. Not strong enough I made a number of stops on my way to and from the pens before I gaining the required strength to move the loads with ease. Additional tasks included preparing the food, killing, plucking and cleaning fowl. In the mornings we released the livestock from their houses and shut them away safely at dusk.

The workforce consists of, Joey, Michel Fahey and myself.

Then there was *The Boss*, Joe McBride an unforgettable character. Seen from a distance with a short squat body he appeared all arms and legs. His well-worn ill-fitting denim jeans ended well short of large hobnailed boots. Always moving in a hurry the right arm swung wildly out from his body, whilst the left was bent and swung across his front as if to balance and keep him upright. His upper body bunched and fitted into an ill-fitting denim jacket containing buttons always left undone. Seeing him a picture of a Daddy Long Legs springs to mind, with his large hump pushing his jacket sleeves well short of reaching his wrists. A face that was creased and weathered, with eyes squinting as though looking into sunlight. It is a stony, expressionless face, which would be impossible to imagine melting into a smile. His head was covered in a tight mat of close-cropped black hair speckled with grey. He rarely spoke other than to grunt instructions at one of us. We know only to well to keep out of the reach of those long legs, as he has a habit of aiming a kick at us should we get close.

He's accommodated and dines in the Brothers' Quarters. His whole life appeared to revolve around his work on the poultry farm, for he rarely ventured beyond the institution boundaries.

Joey's interest in the livestock, and the work that it involved fired my imagination. I was awake to the farm life all around me; the livestock so content and free. The pure breed's of hen were kept apart in special breeding pens, I came to learn their identity like: Sussex, Rhode Island Red, Wyandotte, Minorca, and the light breeds like the Black, and White Leghorn. Then there were the different breeds of duck like the Aylesbury, Kaki Campbell and Indian Runner.

To complete the list there were turkeys, American Bronze and Whites, Toulouse geese, and the pretty grey white speckled Guinea Hens, with their high-pitched chattering sound, as though they 're saying "go back, go back."

One house located on the farm had the advantage of overlooking the whole area. Mr. Hanley who was old, tall and thin resided there alone. Part of it also served as his office. He could be seen thrice daily as he made his way to meals at the Brothers' quarters. He wore an old battered Fedora hat with the brim pulled down to shade a pallid face, while his cloths hung loose on his gaunt frame. He treaded slowly along, always holding a small, cloth-covered basket of eggs in one hand and a walking stick in the other. On the return journeys it was noticeable the eggs had been a replaced with snacks. Should we cross paths during one of his daily ventures he would neither speak nor appears to notice us. Maybe to him we didn't even exist. McBride and he appeared to work together in the house, what they found to do held little interest for me. They proceeded to meals separately in spite of sharing the same dining area.

The daily sound of the angelus bell was the signal for Joey and I to proceed with the empty swill bin and Hessian sacks to collect waste from the Brothers' kitchen. We pushed the trolley containing a large empty swill bin, which swung loosely on its hinges. As we strolled along the roads to the tradesmen's entrance of the Brothers' quarters, Joey tells me: "On Mondays we visit the farm to collect blood". "Where do we get the blood from?"

"From a cow of course." "Ah go on. Your coding me, everyone knows you get milk from cows, don't ye?"

With a roar of laughter he replied: "Not if they are dead". "How do they die?" I'm intrigued. But Joey closes the subject. "Never mind. You'll see for yourself on Mondays."

On our arrival at the Brothers' kitchen we collected the leftovers. The sacks we filled with the leftover bread and we exchanged our bin for one full of swill. We always moved faster on our return journey in anticipation of the treasures we might find among the swill.

On arrival at the preparation room we would share out the best scraps of the white bread between the three of us. Tilting the swill bin on its hinges we slowly pour the contents into two large galvanised buckets. The steam rose from the bin as I poured; releasing a variety of smells some sweet, some sour. Sour apple peel and potatoes; meat bones covered in gravy.

Joey taught me what to look out for.

"Scoop out that mashed potato, move the other stuff to the side." As we shared the mash and gobbled it up it tastes deliciously smooth and milky. I discovered some bones covered in yellow goo. As I washed the bones under the tap I enquired of Joey what the yellow stuff is.

"God Charlie, You don't know much about food de ya? That's custard". "It's ok for you. You've been here longer than I have".

"Sure you're right, see the lumps of custard? Go easy and separate it from the rest. You'll love it. Boy that's some taste".

To prepare food for the livestock, we mixed the meal, bran, swill and the remainder of the bread. Although I was less than five foot tall I was able to lift the large sacks of chicken meal and the sacks of bran.

Along the wall to the left of the entrance there was a workbench containing three compartments. Each just high enough from the ground to enable us to lean against and to reach across its full width. Using a scoop we unloaded large quantities of meal and bran into our individual sections.

With our shirtsleeves rolled up, we mixed the contents to create a hollow in the centre. Just like preparing a mix of cement. The swill with the bread broken up into pieces was placed in the centre with water. Our hips close to the board, backs bent, we pummelled away mixing with hands and arms only pausing to break up lumps. We scooped the resultant mixture into the large galvanised buckets for delivery to the food troughs of the livestock. I staggered down the path with a loaded bucket in each hand.

"Charlie take a rest now and then. Bend your arms".

"Why do I need to bend me arms?"

I gasp. Joey gives a hoot of laughter.

"A Sure your arms are long enough anyway. Soon your knuckles will be scraping along the ground" The livestock fought and pushed to get at the food before it was out of the bucket, just like the kids on the parade ground at lunch time when there was no controlling Brother present. There was a musical sound of contentment from the hens, as they anticipate their meal.

The ducks by contrast, madly quacking as they begged impatiently for their meal. When it came to noise levels the geese easily topped the league, screaming incessantly for their food. Joey never warned me about feeding the geese. The first time I went to feed them; he had already released them. They came rushing towards me half-running part flying, led by a large gander with his neck stiff and straight. He wasn't joining in the chorus of the high-pitched communal screech but wildly hissing, intent on attacking me to protect his flock. He hissed and pecked at me as if to say, "Get out of here". I dropped the buckets and ran. The gander ran past the buckets then turned to join his flock, who were by then eating from the buckets. Joey was creased up with laughter at the spectacle. As the gander approached the buckets, he exhibited a threatening pose. With a deft movement Joey grabbed him by the upper neck and lowered its head to the ground, holding him at a distance from his body to avoid injury.

"You see those wings? They can break your leg, so this is how you deal with him"

The turkeys were less of a problem to feed. They just keep shouting "gobble, gobble, gobble" in a high pitched voice. As they ate their food with their head nodding while the food went down their gullets. The cock pumped himself up to display his beautiful fanned tail and strutted around monitoring his flock as if to say "I'm the Boss here".

Having fed the livestock, we prepared to water them. Joey continued with snippets of advice: "Keep very alert when mixing the food, McBride's sneaky. He'll lash out with those big boots and smash you against the mixing boards".

In response to my query as to why McBride would do this, he continued: "I expect he'll enjoy hurting you twice with one kick. A hobnailed boot in the behind, then crash your hips against the boards".

"Joey have you ever seen him smile?"

"No but, he's maybe got notin to smile about".

My first few weeks at fulltime work flew by, it had been hard work but rewarding I also ate well. How wonderful to witness fluffy chicks and the proud mother clucking round them encouragingly. There were also the goslings and ducklings, so small you could cover them completely with one hand. How vigilant the mother watched over them as they swam happily in the concrete pool. Observing them I think how wonderful it would be to swim free like them. The gander is better than a guard dog when it comes to protecting his charges from harm.

As Christmas got closer we worked late into the night.

We had chickens and ducks to kill by wringing their neck. The turkeys and geese McBride killed with a knife. We plucked, cleaned and prepared the birds. Whose table these birds were destined for we knew not, nor could we comprehend the purpose of our work. There's a technique we learned to remove and discard the legs by cutting the skin, snapping the leg bone and pulling the leg with ligaments free. There were gizzards, livers, hearts, and necks to cut, clean and pack into the cavity.

It felt good to be working late with the lights on and the warmth of the paraffin oil heater. This I found special about Christmas, lots of work and a resultant sense of achievement. We collected, and bagged different colours and sizes of feathers. The smell of the oil heater mingled with the blood and waste parts of the fowl brought a festive air into our lives.

We trudged our weary way back to the dormitories in the dark, content in the knowledge of having done a good day's work. The smell of the dead foul hung about us and wisps of feathers clung to our hair and cloths. Lice from the fowl found a new refuge on our bodies.

On entering the dormitory I felt like falling straight into bed. The stench of the birds' waste matter clinging to my hands compelled me to wash in hot water first. With only cold water at the farm to wash in, at the day's end we still carried around the smell of chicken food and dead livestock, which has impregnated our skin.

Christmas day we were allowed a little longer dinner time for which we looked forward to each year: ham, roast, peas, pudding and wine (lemonade). These four named foods, mouthed each year were rolled into one word, which became synonymous with Christmas, as we rubbed our hands together in anticipation of that very special meal.

With our Christmas work completed, other work must carry on as normal, except that only we *nobodies* were still in the Institution over the festive season. The farming and poultry trades required us to carry on work as normal every day of the year. It was rare indeed for City fellow to choose these trades. We've the rare white bread for our meals.

In the late evenings after work we played board in the empty classrooms, games such as checkers and snakes and ladders.

It's a Monday, which meant a visit to the farmyard. Joey, Michel and I, each carry a large galvanised bucket as we saunter up the road. Joey tells me we're going to collect the blood from the cow. In the cobblestone yard there were two men holding ropes attached to a frightened cow's neck. The cow oozes fear as it senses its fate and pulls back, from the ropes. Both men were leaning back on the tightened rope to hold its neck steady. The cow was held still as a third man placed a cold black lead colt between its eyes. There was the sound of a thud rather than the bang I expected. The cow staggered then slumped to the ground. There were still slight tremors from the beast as the farm hands moved it on to its back. One of them produced a gleaming sharp knife and proceeds to cut a piece of hide from the chest. Joey placed his bucket by the wound.

"Charlie, Get up on its belly, when the man plunges the knife in you start jumping up and down". Instructed Joey.

Up I climbed gripping a front leg; Michel held my other hand to steady me as I jump. The warm red liquid gushed forth, followed by a steady flow into the tilted bucket.

"Steady up Charlie, the bucket's near full".

Michel hurriedly switched to buckets.

The performance was repeated until the flow of red liquid was reduced to a trickle. By the time we struggled back with our loads, the blood was already starting to congeal. We poured the thick, dark red, still warm liquid into the centre of the dry mix of bran and meal. The speed by which the birds' gobbled the mixture indicated it was much to their liking.

During the first summer at work I experienced a wonderful afternoon of freedom. The weather was warm with intermittent showers, our afternoon work finished and McBride was on his day off. Joey offered to show me where the main supplies of straw and hay were stored. I didn't hesitate to follow him over the wall and out on to a public country road. As we strolled along the road we were caught in a down pore allowing us to enjoy a good soaking. The road was deserted as people sheltered in a short line of thatched whitewashed cottages on one side of the road. When we reached a barn inside a field, we both dashed in flinging off our soaked shirts and rolled in the hay, then treated our young bodies to the warmth of sun. As the setting of the sun it was time to return to house the livestock for the night. With our shirts still damp we walked back along the road with a faked confidence so as not to attract attention. There were some women out fetching water from the roadside pumps. An old man sat by his cottage door with his collie dog by his side enjoying the evening sun.

As if to reinforce we were not runaways, I reached to pet the dog. Quick as a flash and without a sound from it or the man, it bit my hand.

Although my hand was bleeding we carried on our way as though nothing happened, for fear of being reported.

One evening in the late autumn of my second year we had just housed the livestock for the night when Joey and Michel spring a surprise. "Charlie, Meet us in the straw shed after work, and make sure McBride has set off for his evening meal before you come" As I entered the straw shed Michel told me to close the door and pull my straw bail close to the heater. Laid out on three bails was a feast of white bread, apples and eggs. A burning paraffin oil heater was being used to boil the eggs in a battered tin. My friends proudly smiled at their ingenuity in preparing such a feast. "Where did you get the apples?"

"We climbed on the roof which leads to the garden wall, and bartered some bread for apples with one of the garden workers Michel knows"

When I asked Joey why he didn't use eggs in exchange. Joey smiled explaining: "I don't think eggs would have been safe to chuck over the wall.

Besides timing's all-important. They have to have a lookout. Anyways they've notin to boil the eggs in".

We settled down to a feast of hard-boiled eggs, soft white bread and sweet, juicy apples. It was one of the best feasts I'd ever had. I'd ate more eggs in two consecutive evening's sittings than in each of the past five years. The normal ration was just two eggs each year at Easter time.

I knew the food was stolen and had thereby committed a sin. I felt no sense of guilt; in fact I'd wished we'd did this during my first year's working. As we sat chatting and sipping water I voiced my concerns about what might lay ahead for my future. "I'm very scared about working for someone that won't keep me on, what if he or she sends me back? You know what happened with that one who was sent back, getting a *mooner* and the treatment?"

"Charlie, are you sure you don't have anyone on the outside?" Joey's voice sounded kind and caring.

"I don't think so. No one's ever asked about me. Can't see why anyone would want me, the Brothers always say I'm no good, never getting the correct answers. I was sent me here from Kilkenny and no one came while I was there."

"Have a talk with Brother Ambrose. He's found a number of fellows' relatives, who then came to collected them when they were due out" he explained.

"Something always puzzles me, why would parents not want their children?" Michel replied after lengthy consideration.

"Lots of reasons, some just don't want kids, others lose them, while others can't manage and want to forget about them". I ponder this information.

"It doesn't matter now, as they'd just be strangers. If someone came for me I'd be scared to go with him or her. Anyway I'm too old to need a Mammy or Da. It might be better to go with someone who's happy with my work and won't beat me just for the fun of it or send me back."

"What do you mean too old? What do you know about a Mammy?"

Joey seemed to be a bit of a dreamer. It was Michel who agreed with me. "If parents came for me they'd be strangers. So whoever gets me, an' if they're not happy with me, I'll run far, far away, even out of the country an' they'll never catch me. One of the Dublin fellers was telling me the Garda were after his Da so he skipped off to England, I could do that. I know I'm never, ever coming back here".

"Well I know the mother hen stays and looks after her chicks. Feeds them and let's them snuggle under her wings. And how about the cat in the shed with the kittens? Look how she cares for them. When the young grow up they go off on their own." There was a note of despair in my voice. "They're animals. People are not like that" Joey's voice was hard and bitter. "I don't care, they should be. How about you two, aren't you worried?" "Brother Ambrose already told me there was no one outside for me. Whoever I'm farmed out to, I'll work so hard they will be pleased and give me money an' I'll save and become rich"

Brother Ambrose was the oldest person I've ever known. He must have had no home other than the Institution also had no job that I was aware of. Leaving church late each evening he shuffled his way across the parade ground, staying close to the railings by the football pitch. He might as well have been a ghost for all the notice anyone took of him. Where he went to each day? I never discovered. His head was bent from the neck and stuck permanently in that position. His head and neck were as smooth and polished as marble. He and Clumba (the oldest teacher) were the only Brothers who held no fear for any of us. It looked as though a puff of wind would knock him over.

I decided to approach him with my concerns.

"Brother, Can I ask you something?"

He turned his head up to one side, his mouth opens, exuding foul breath. His tone expressed irritation.

"Yes boy what is it you wish?"

Perhaps he thought I'd come to mock him like some of the other boys.

"I was wondering if it was possible if you could find out if I belonged to someone on the outside and who might want to have me. I'm due for release soon."

His voice was slow and halting: "I'll see what can be done, I can't promise anything, as there are some boys who have no one at all. And then there're other boys who're so bad no one would wish to take them".

Withdrawing a notebook and pencil from inside his food stained cassock, with gasped breath: "Well boy, what's your name and age?"

"I'm Charlie Rice, I'm not sure about age, but I must be nearing sixteen because I've worked two Christmas'".

He smiled as he shuffled on his way, now I awaited in the hope of something good to happen.

I had taken Joey's advice to keep alert whenever McBride was hovering about while I'm mixed food. So far I've been fast enough to dodge his attempted kicks and ran outside only to return to complete my work once he'd left. But of late he's managed to hit his target more often. On one occasion I felt the full force of McBride's boot up my backside sending me crashing against the board. He was so quiet; the only sound was the thud as my hips crashed against the counter and my spontaneous yelp of pain. He carried on as though nothing happened, while I was bend in pain. The hurt had increased my determination to do something about his kicking. No matter how alert I became with my back to him, he still managed to catch me.

He arrived just as I was starting to prepare the foodstuff for mixing. Knowing I would spend time bent over the mixing bench facing the wall with my hands up to my elbows, mixing away.

He was also aware that I was alert to his games and so it became a game of hit or miss.

In deciding I was not fast enough I had to admit he was wining by making more hits than misses. I decided to enlist Joey's help.

"Would you try to see if you could catch me with a kick on the backside?" "Sure I'll kick you if it 'ill bring some sense into your thick head". "Stop laughing Joey. It's not funny, I'm fed up with McBride kicking me and I want to stop him." "How will my kicking you stop him?" "I want to practice trying catching you by the heel as you kick".

Joey readily agreed to a daily practice. In no time I became expert at catching his heel before he made contact: "I'm now ready to teach that fecken Humpty Dumpy a lesson". Joey expresses a wish to be out of sight as he spectates. I didn't have long to wait for the game to begin. I was mixing away, keeping my hands close to the front of the bench as McBride entered the room. I sensed his presence behind me as he moved from my vision. By now I was ready sharp and alert. As I glanced to one side I could see his foot leave the ground. Whipping my hand back, I caught his heel. In one movement I raised my hand and let go for him to crash to the ground on his hump.

In a flash I was running scared out of there for dear life, increasing the pace down the road and out of the poultry farm, with Joey's laughter ringing in my ears. I stopped to catch my breath, and rerun the scene in my mind. McBride rocking on his hump I sniggered for a second, Joey had nearly wet himself with laughter. I saw Joey later in the parade ground, as it was early finishing time of year. The winter evenings were drawing in and I knew my time here is nearing its end, that I must be nearing sixteen years old. Now I was too scared to return to the poultry farm.

"Joey I can't go back there. I know I've done wrong but I'm too scared to go back. What 'm I to do?" As always Joey came up with the answer.

"In the morning when the farm boys line up for work just join in. There're so many of them, one more won't be noticed. McBride got what was coming to him, but ah janie it was hilarious".

I still felt guilty for what I had done to McBride. Think he must have been a very lonely man with his affliction and I had just added to his miseries.

Joey turned out to be right. No one noticed I'd joined the other farm workers on their way to work each morning. During my final weeks I worked in the fields picking potatoes, milking the cows and cleaning out their sheds. I was never to see Joey again he just seemed to vanish like a mist, there were no farewells, or good byes. I can't ever recall saying good byes to any one, but then such sentiments were absent from our lives.

Nobody appeared to notice my non-appearance at the poultry farm. I can't never forget Joey and I sincerely hope he found that rich happy and successful life, he deserved.

When next I broached Brother Ambrose on his daily shuffle he informed me: "There is someone interested in you and you will find out in good time". I am overjoyed to learn someone might want me, and yet curious as to whom it could be and why me. Nobody had ever been interested in me before. After thanking him, he started telling me things I did not understand. But then that is what grown ups do, they don't teach though they think they do. I knew what he was talking about, at least I though I did when he said: "Don't ever force yourself to go to the toilet, if you do, you'll be committing a mortal sin". I though to myself, "That's a stupid thing to say you go to the toilet when you want to. There's no need to force yourself. That's like telling me to 'shut my mouth and eat my food. Or get off that wall, if you fall and break your leg don't come running to me', *as if I would ever run to a Brother*. I wondered if he was OK in the head?".

It was late September when I was summed to the main Brother's office. It must have had something to do with my future fate, for I'd never been there before. A Brother held the door open inviting me into the office. There was a small neat woman standing facing me on the other side of the room. I'd heard the door close as the Brother moved to my left, breaking the silence as he turned and introduced me to the woman: "This is your mother". Dumbstruck with nothing to say. My eyes focus on the paper cone clasped in the woman's hands. I'm left wondering what kind of sweets are in it and what they must taste like. I'd seen such cones before which the parents brought on visiting days for their kids. The woman interrupted my thoughts. "What's your name?" Nervously I tell her, "Charlie Rice." She appears surprised, and looks enquiringly at the Brother. "Are you sure you've got the right one?" Now I'm worried, I won't get the sweets after all. I was aware there was another fellow in the band by the same name, but he was called Johnnie Rice.

If I were a bold enough fellow I'd have said, "Well you tell me what me name is, I'm always being told things, I only know what I'm told".

The Brother comes to the rescue, "What is your number young man?".

Ah, I'm relieved, that's easy, and with pride I spout "11536 Brother".

"That's your boy all right, I'll leave you two alone for a while".

Talking more to herself than me, she mumbled: "You look like him all right". Her lack of height allowed me to snatch a look of disappointment as she seized me up. I sensed maybe she'd changed her mind and was finding it an effort to accept me. Joey was more a friend than this stranger was.

"Your name is Patrick not Charlie. Do you understand?"

This was very confusing and unsettling. I felt uncomfortable and wished to be out of there, but not before I got my hands on those sweets. I'd have loved to snatch the packet and to have made a run for it before she could whacked me. I was trapped in the room with a strange woman.

"How do you like it here?" There she was again in addition to telling me my name she's got another question. I tell her, "OK". She hands me the sweets, muttering something about getting them for me. As I snatched at them and back off, she reached to touch me. My whole body is repelled and silently screaming : "Get away don't touch me", as I backed away.

"Are you sure you're all right?" In a strained voice I repeated that I was. Now I've got what I want I just wish to be gone from there. Oh God, she's started talking again. "I'll be coming back in a week or so to take you out of here. What do you think of that?". What I think is, you ask question after question. That's all you can come out with. But I tell her, OK just to be rid of her. I don't want to see her again but I had no say in what happens to me. At last she was leaving. As she made for the door I give her a wide berth, while she informed the Brother she'd be back in a week or so to *collect* me.

The next time I saw the woman was a visiting day having been instructed to join the other fellows on the parade ground. The shock of being told I will no longer be known as Charlie had set in.

Faceless people insisted I was to follow this strange woman out into an equally strange world. In addition the woman has decided to change my name to one I'd never feel comfortable with.

To add to the confusion a younger woman accompanied the older one on the next visit. The younger one introduce herself; "I'm Margaret, your sister". The girl, I learnt later, is about four years older than I.

She had dark hair, light blue eyes, and pail complexion. Small and pretty but not beautiful, She had a nice scented smell about her. She smiled and extended her hand: "Hello Paddy" So now I'm Paddy! Taking her hand I shyly said "Hello." They'd brought me food as all the other parents had over the years. The pair of them talked at length about plans they'd made for me when I was to leave. There were of little interest to me as I gobble down the food they brought. Right then food meant everything to me.

I missed the daily feed at the poultry farm and the absence of Joey's supply of white bread. I knew nothing much of the world beyond the walls of this school. I was unconcerned about what would happen to me in the future.

I drifted along like a discarded piece of paper in the wind and become attached to anyone who'd take control. Up to then the only decision I'd had to make was easy, to work on the poultry farm. All my needs had been taken care of while in the custody of the Brothers. I knew when and how often I must do everything and I understood this world.

On the day of my departure the woman and Margaret came to collect me to take home. It was just another number move in my life, the third. There were no farewells or excitement as I tagged along obediently with these two strange women. Neither they nor I were aware of how stunted my developmental levels were.

Although Charlie might no longer exist to these women, he would always remain part of me. It was the name I responded to for sixteen years.

Now, whenever I am asked my name there is always a pause while I decide to reply with, "Pat, Paddy or Patrick". Often it's with my surname.

As for the Christian Brothers I believe they carried out their duties to the best of their limited capabilities. I'm inclined to think of them as the Para Military Wing of the Catholic Church in

Ireland. They were incapable of providing the special care these children required, it is therefore fitting I should forgive them for they knew not what they did.

CHAPTER FIVE

My Prison Within

After six years in Artane, I was what the official documents record being 'disposed off'. From where I had been conditioned to respond to orders I was entering a strange new one world. Free but didn't feel free, I was somewhat scared and lost. The clothes I wore were my Sunday best, these comprised all my worldly possessions. There was a shirt with a collar, my first pair of long trouser, a vest (waistcoat) socks, boots and jacket.

Only early this year (2006) did I discover the date of my release, the seventh of October 1947. Back then days and dates were of little or no account. The following day would have been my sixteenth birthday. Along with me, my newfound sister and the Mammy all were unconscious of that fact. It wasn't surprising, with not having contact with me in the proceeding sixteen years. It would take many years for me to adjust and become familiar with the customs of celebrating birthdays and other important anniversaries throughout the year.

There were no new guidelines to follow other than those set by these women. As I tagged along with them I had some fears and concerns about my ability to adjust to this strange New World. We boarded a double-decker bus filled with men and women of all ages, and even boys and girls are mixed together. People are chattering away like the livestock I had tended. The smells of pipe tobacco, cigarettes, perfume and stale sweat all mix in competition, the constant hubbub of conversation evoked a strange sensation of newfound freedom.

The woman Margaret called "Mammy" sat beside me, whispered: "If anyone speaks to you remember never to mention 'Artane'. Forget you were ever there. D'ya understand"?

Nodding my head vigorously her look of nervous concern was enough to make me promise to forget I was ever there. In time I would learn with good reason to remain silent about my former home, where the courts committed children, for breaking the law or for having a parent already in prison. Indeed there were seventeen reasons under the 1908 and 1924 Acts to place children in the custody of those so-called carers.

We alighted from the bus in the centre of Dublin City to a deafening level of noise from cars, buses, horse and carts, and paperboys shouting their wares. The names of the two papers were rolled into one; Herald or Mail in a singsong fashion that sounded just like one word. People walking by, others were dashing in every direction. I was awestruck and fearful of getting lost. The voice of the Mammy snapped me out of my wondering state:

"Will you stop gawking at people, and shut your gob"

I stuck close to the pair of them as we crossed the busy Caple Street. The rich mealy smell of porter, which wafted from the city pubs, filled the air long before coming upon them. One such a pub was located at the corner of Little Mary Street, a short narrow grimy back street.

The green door of number eighteen, of a tenement dwelling, was open, inviting us along its dark narrow corridor. It was good to get out of the sharp cold weather. The building reeked of stale cooking, soiled nappies, unwashed bodies and tobacco. Our footsteps resounded on the bare, well-trodden wooden stairs as we ascended the narrow stairway to the third floor.

A small window coated in a film of grime dimly light the landings of each floor. On the third floor Margaret unlocked one of two doors to a single room which looked out on the street below. The room contained the barest essentials to get by.

"Well Paddy this is our home, you'll be sharing it with Joe and me. There's a mattress on the floor over there for ya".

The prospect of staying here did nothing to raise my already low spirits, at least the worn wooden floor was well scrubbed. In addition to the double bed there was a table, a cupboard, a three-seat couch, and my mattress on the floor. An oil lamp was the only source of light, as there was no electricity supply to the building. What little cooking took place was carried out on the small fireplace using either the one frying, or saucepan. On the windowsill stood their most prized possession, a small wireless powered by a larger battery, which required topping up and charging at the nearest garage.

It proved difficult to start the fire at this time of year, and 1947 was then the coldest winter on record. The damp wood for the fire we forage from around the city streets. On very rare occasions when Joe backed a winner at the bookies we had the luxury of burning turf or a little coal. Water had to be carried in the all-purpose bucket from the communal yard below at the rear of the building. The toilets in the yard served the needs of all the building's residence.

Margaret and her Mother chatted away as though I didn't exist. Snippets of the conversation, which prove of interest I filter out, like the talk of food. There was little option I knew I had but allow these people to control all aspects of my daily life. Before the Mammy left, my "sister" reassured her: "Don't worry Mammy I'll look after him and get him out to work each day." Turning to me the Mammy said she'd see me sometime next week, but that held little or no interest for me. Later I met Joe, Margaret's husband he was a lean handsome man of swarthy complexion, with even white teeth and slick black wavy hair. His clothes were tread bear while his shoes were down at the heel. He had a ready smile and a cheery disposition, a happy go lucky type. A cobbler by trade, but didn't appear to be practicing then, yet he enjoyed a drink, smoke and a gamble. His relaxed manner when dealing with me I found a nice change. He asked about the Mammy and how I was settling in. I explained I didn't really know her and mentioned she was returning next week.

During the Mammy's weekend visits I listened to the women as they talked picking up snippets of information. As they chatted away, I was never drawn into the conversations, I would have had little of value to add. It was as though I was a newborn in this world, and my past sixteen years had no relevance to present life.

From their talks and through Joe I discovered Margaret had an older sister Phyllis, whom she had not seen in years. She was about seven years older than I, and lived with her father's two sisters. She also worked in the city, and by the way they spoke of her, it was easy to gather there was no love lost between them. There was no mention of a father, except once when the Mammy reminisced about him in happier times. From her conversations I was left with the impression she liked dressing up and partying, a bit of a butterfly.

When addressing me it did not strike me as strange that the Mammy never used terms of endearment. Could it be she was disappointed in what she had gotten after waiting sixteen years? In turn I found no cause for bitterness towards her. Indeed there was a lack of any feeling towards her. These people were complete strangers, I felt under no obligation to them.

Only in time would I develop the ability to freely express my feelings without fear of punishment. I'm sure Margaret didn't bargain on getting a brother incapable of thinking for himself. Her frustration with me manifested itself by screaming, yelling and dishing out the odd clout.

One day as I made my way downstairs to the toilet, I stopped at the bottom landing. Looking idly through the window I saw a woman squatting with her skirt raised. She was peeing on the yard floor and I wondered why she couldn't stand up and pee like everyone else?

My first job I found myself working in a factory as a cleaner, mostly sweeping the floors. How I managed to be working there I never knew as I passed my days in a trance. The factory girls mocked me. Their gibes were wasted on me, for I was only too aware I was of little consequence. Sleeping in the same cloths I became oblivious to the unkempt figure I must have cut. With proper washing facilities and change of clothing I may have learned to make myself look halfway decent.

But that was just a pipe dream. From my weekly packet of five shillings I received six pence pocket money which I spend on broken biscuits. My animal instincts took over when it came to food, greedily and secretly I wolfed down every crumb. I had never learned to share nor would I for many years and only then by observing the habits of others. Most evenings I hung around Moore Street, the fruit and vegetable market, where the stallholders could be heard hawking their wares in a rich Dublin accent. "Penny each the apples and oranges." I waited until the stalls closed in the late evening and under cover of darkness I could get my fill of discarded food, scavenged from bins or gutter. Walking along slowly I dipped quickly and slipped the scavenged food into a pocket. Anything on the ground was fair game, but I didn't wish to be seen, as the shame was too great. Dark back allies were good places to feast on my gains. It helped to keep the pangs of hunger at bay.

It was not long before I found living with Margaret and Joe so unbearable that I decided to do a bunk. But the fear of being returned to 'Artane' made it imperative that I first find a new and better-paid job. As it was, my fears might well have been unfounded. Unknown to me then, under the heading on the official documents it reads: Ultimate Disposal on the 7 October 1947: .... "To his Mother, 4, Florence Street S. C. Rd. Dublin for employment at Western Hotel, S. C. Rd. Dublin. Page Boy @ 10/= p. w."

A visit to the Unemployment Bureau in the beginning of December '47 resulted in my being employed as an apprentice cabinetmaker with Myers of Marlboro Street. Now I earned a pound a week, enough to save towards buying some new cloths. As an apprentice I spent most of my time out on the streets collecting and delivering completed cabinets and parts. The mode of transport was a horse and cart. The old driver knew every street and back lane of dirty old Dublin. On one journey he pointed out a Boys' Home in Middle Abbey Street not far from Little Mary Street. I think he sensed it might better suit my needs if I could manage to gain entry to the Home. Or could it be the odour of a retched unwashed youth accompanying him on the daily rounds? The home was a shelter for homeless young men working and living in the city.

My decision to apply for entry into the home was hastened when Margaret flew into a rage at me for the umpteenth time, at my term of speech when referring to the Mammy."You will not refer to your Mother as "she" and "her". She's not something the cat brought in; you will call her Mam or Mammy".

This proved to be the fuse for me to explode with rage:

"I will never call anyone Mam or Mammy, I will not, never, never". Her reaction was to physically attacking me. Why can't she understand? The word Mom, Mammy or Mother is only reserved for very special people, not for just any woman. Shortly after that episode the Mammy, Margaret and Joe were out of my life forever when I successfully gained entry to the Boys' Home. There were perhaps twenty young men living at the home in Middle Abbey Street. Their ages ranged from sixteen to around twenty-five, and most, if not all had been in the "care" of the Christian Brothers. Board and food at half a crown a week was very good value. The greatest benefit was being among young men from a similar background who were considering their life's future options. Most were hoping to join the armed forces, in Ireland, Britain, or the U.S. I had not gained sufficient confidence to even contemplate the USA. Experiences of

Irish institutions were not something I yearned to repeat. It seemed my future would rest with the British Forces. But that opportunity I learnt, must wait until I was old enough.

By mid January 1948 I'd changed jobs once again and found work just across the street from The Home. I was now a messenger boy for Bradshaw's Wholesale Motor Parts and earning one pound a week. It proved to be better, now I had a bike to get around the city, no more need to waste money on buses. Whenever I got on a bus I was consumed with panic, it meant asking a stranger for a ticket. What if I got off at the wrong stop? I still lacked the confidence to ask. Did I look and act like someone who's been in 'Artane'?

I had the same problem buying items in shops, it came as a relief to share the company of one of the lads from The Home when out shopping.

According to the rules of the Home we had to vacate, each morning by nine o'clock, when it was locked until five in the evening. Most of us worked a six and a half-day week, which resulted in us spending little time at the home, except for breakfast, evenings and weekends.

With plenty of free time I explored the city streets. One summer evening as I wandered along

Gardener Street I passed a children's' playground and noticed a child on a swing. She was wearing no knickers. How surprised and shocked I was to see she had no *Mickey*. So *that* was the difference between boys and girls', life then was full of such surprises.

It was about this time that I decided out of curiosity, to track down the older sister Phyllis, they had talked about. Maybe she had a nice home and with a little luck I might by able to scrounge a place to stay. I'd remembered the Mammy mentioning that she had a good job as a Colour Matcher with Smith's and Heyworth, a Hosiery factory in Patrick Street.

I waited on the opposite side of the street to the factory gates, intent on following her home. Although I had never met, nor seen a photograph of her, the thought never entered my mind that this might present a problem. As the workforce poured through the factory gates my eyes lit on a slim, very pretty dark haired girl. The hair was curly with a parting down the centre. She had a pale completion with high cheekbones and was smartly dressed. I know not how, but instinctively I knew she was my sister.

Phyllis Rice

Keeping my distance I trailed her for almost a mile until she stopped on the sidewalk to open a door with a latchkey. I approached the door and stood trying to compose myself, thinking through my next move as I waited. After an age of indecision, I knocked on the door. There she was, standing in front of me, feeling uneasy, I lowered my eyes to contemplate my scruffy boots.

"Yes what do you want?"

"I'm Paddy, Paddy Rice, your brother".

I answered in a small timid voice.

There was a long pause, and then the voice of a woman from upstairs broke the silence, asking who it was at the door:

"It's Paddy my brother".

The voice instructed her to invite me in. Upstairs were two older women, whom I learned were her aunts Madge and Dolly, her father's sisters. They lived in this flat above a shop. It consisted of a lounge, kitchen and other rooms I never saw into. The two women talked a lot about the family and I responded to their questions quietly, mostly with a "Yes" or "No". It appeared that there was some rift in the family, which was none of my concern. No one was ever exactly overjoyed to see me, I always felt like an intruder. Could it have been I was so tainted by my "time served" in 'Artane'? As I left the flat I still had the feeling of being very much alone in the world, but would have liked to get a chance to prove worthy of having a sister like Phyllis.

By the late summer of 1948 I had moved on once again to a new job at the Irish Bankers' Club, in Stephen's Green, a male only member club. Two nice old ladies ran the club, Mrs Ferguson and Mrs Henderson, I think they must have felt a degree of sympathy for me when I told them I didn't have a home of my own. I worked under the supervision of two older male employees. There were also two women workers, the younger one I believed to be in her mid twenties, a Miss Wilmot. With the exception of the older man we all lived in the upstairs of the premises. At last, for the first time in my life, I had my very own bedroom. Tim Clarke (the younger man) and I performed the daily chores, which consisted of cleaning the rooms, lighting the fires, the washing-up and learning to wait on tables.

Work was mainly in the mornings when some club members visited for breakfast and cleaning up after the late nights. There was a short burst of work at midday leaving us afternoons free. Late evenings and weekends were the busiest times when most of the members frequented the club.

As the weeks and months passed I felt restless with a vague feeling there was something missing to my life. I was unconscious of having passed my seventeenth birthday. At evening meal times I visited the Boys Home to keep up to date on the latest goings on. It also helped me to get a wider perspective of the diverse options open to me from likeminded fellows. There was a strong need to feel part of the pack in their small world.

I needed an anchor, as I appeared to float among many strangers.

Phyllis, though she did not know it provided me with a sense of belonging, so I persisted with the occasional visits to her home.

My co-worker Clarke seems to find some of my idiosyncrasies simpleminded and funny, such as licking my plate, or scooping up crumbs to eat after a meal, habits hard to shed.

Christmas of '48 was going to be very special; I now felt free of anyones control. Walking the streets of the city, the lights, glitter and decorations in the shops cheered me. Seeing people scurrying home loaded with shopping and gifts, I was swept along in the Christmas fantasise. Christmas Eve I was so excited as I hung up my socks on the brass head rail of my bed and found it difficult sleep wondering what Santa would bring me overnight.

Early morning I was full of excitement, my eyes fell upon the beautifully wrapped gift at the end of my bed. Carefully I unwrapped my very first Christmas present which proved to be a lovely pair of socks. There was no indication were it came from. I took it for granted as being part of the Christmas spirit. Now for my socks on the bedpost. They were both full. When I emptied the contents onto the bed, I was shocked to discover a mess of dust and cinders. Someone had filled my socks with cinders, wild with rage, I picked up my life's first and only present with it's wrapping and throw them on the fire. This kind of cruelty I didn't understand and my reaction was instinctive. My stunted developmental levels must have been so evident causing one of the staff to take advantage. I was unconcerned as to who had cruelly crushed such childish innocence. My chief suspect was Clarke, as I couldn't imagine a woman being capable of such a cruel act.

From that moment on I forged a set of unshakeable values that no one would ever take from me.

In the first few months of the New Year I decided to apply to enlist in the British Forces. With advice and assistance from some of the lads at the Boys' Home I learnt I had to be at least seventeen and a half years old before I could apply to enlist. I also required a copy of my birth certificate as proof of my age. My birth certificate provided me with the father's Christian name, registered as Sylvester, and Mother's as Ellen, maiden name Doyle, both of number one, North

King Street, Dublin. My date of birth 8 October 1931 and father's profession was registered as Motor Driver (Bus Driver). Now I had a date to aim for I could start the proceedings of joining the service of my choice, the Royal Air Force.

The first problem surfaced in mid March. The requirement for those under the age of eighteen was a Guardian's signed permission. With my mind made up to enlist as soon as possible, I wasn't prepared to wait until I was eighteen. Since it had been over a year since severing all contact with the 'Mammy' I was left with but one option. That was to seek out my Father and convince him to approve my application.

As expected my first port of call, North King Street drew a blank. I failed to understand that only the very rich possessed a telephone in their homes in the 1940's. Entering a public phone booth with plenty of pennies in my pocket I began telephoning the listed Rice's. Not surprisingly I drew a blank. In that era both the postal and telephone services of Ireland were under one management. Thus I sought the operator's assistance in gaining the required information. Initially she refused saying it was against regulations to divulge such private information. This called for desperate measures so

I pleaded: " Please miss, My Daddy and Mammy split up many years ago and I'm not long out of care, I've no place to stay, and I've only a few pennies. All I'm asking is to see if me Daddy will sign the permission for me to join the forces". "What about your Mammy, can't she help you?" "No, she doesn't want me." It was a last desperate try.

"I'm not supposed to do this, so don't mention I told you".

I tracked down the address the she gave me, it was a corporation house like many in the area. A small dapper man answered my knock on the door. I introduced myself, after a formal handshake he invited me into the parlour. He was neat and tidy with a straight stub of a moustache and swept back thinning dark hair. From the background I could hear the voices of children. He closed the door before asking how I was, then he came straight to the point: "Is there something I can do for you?"

"As I'm under eighteen I was hoping you would sign this application for me   to join the RAF?" "Why can't your mother sign?" "I've no contact with her there's only you, otherwise I'll have to wait until I'm eighteen when I won't need any ones permission. I don't want to wait"

"O.K. give it here, if that's what you wish, your welcome"

I was so happy to have completed my quest.

He enquired further about me. Where was I staying, was I working? We talked only of the present and no other mention of the Mammy or my sisters. When we hit a pregnant silence he lit a cigarette. Opening the door he introduced me to his children and a woman called May. She was taller than my Father, a non-descript, round motherly type with large glasses.

"This is your half brother Paddy; there's Robby, Raymond, Joe, Christy and baby Marie".

They looked pleased to see me and seemed well fed and clothed. The house and family was as I imagined a home would be. On taking my leave of them he wished me luck and told me I was always welcome. The need to take up his offer just might arise then I'd hold him to it.

With his signed permission I was on my way to England. From then on I never considered rejection or failure, and was prepared to accept anything the RAF had to offer me. With good reason I recorded my Father as my next of kin, and his address as my place of abode on the enlistment forms. To admit to having been in Industrial Schools I felt best that left unsaid. Children were committed there by the courts, having fallen foul of the law, such as for *mithching* (failing to attend school) under the School Attendance Act 1926-1968. Some other examples being, a child under twelve, charged with an offence punishable in the case of an adult by penal servitude may be sent to an Industrial School.

A child, having a parent whom does not exercise proper guardianship. Children were detained until aged sixteen.

After almost a month of medical and other tests at the RAF Station in Co. Antrim, I managed to scrape past the basic Math and English tests.

This result in me being offered the lowest grade trade available, *Messing Orderly/Batman/ Waiter*, which I was willing to accept as a start to my first step on the ladder of life.

On the second of May 1949 I swore allegiance in oath to King George the Sixth and Great Britain.

CHAPTER SIX

Innocents Abroad

Strange how I appear to be unable to access my memory bank relating to early journeys between Institutions and the one to England. It must have been by boat. There were twelve of us in all, seven from Southern Ireland the others from the Northern arrived at RAF Cardington for basic training. The Camp appeared to contain about the same number of men as that of Artane. Most were doing their National Service, the rest of us were referred to as regulars and were generally from poorer backgrounds.

We Irish out numbered the other men we were billeted with, an arrangement doomed to failure. Fights broke out between the Northerners' and Southerners' over what appeared to be irreconcilable differences between Orangemen and Republicans. I failed to see the sense or understood the dispute, in spite of my indoctrination in Republican history. The past for me was dead and buried. Complaints from the other men resulted in our dispersal to other billets thus solving the Irish problem. Niall Quinn and I were the only Irish left in our billet.

My introduction to Service life was a wonderfully exciting experience. Being well fed with three wholesome meals a day in addition to being paid. We were issued with all manner unfamiliar items of clothing: such as vests you wore under your shirt. Up to then what I'd known as a vest was a waistcoat. Later in life while working and living with Americans I discovered a vest was part of a three-piece suit, as I had known it to be. My new most prized item of equipment was the Lee Enfield rifle. It hung on cloths hooks above my bed waiting for its every facet to be explored like a new toy.

In addition to clothing and equipment I was given the rank of A/C2 and an identity card with a service number I was instructed to remember.

Basic training was great fun. With years of drill behind me on the parade ground at 'Artane' I was about to be put through a similar routine. Having shed the shackles of fear I tested the patience of a Corporal Noble, the Drill Instructor to breaking point. On one occasion Noble enquired into my tardy behaviour by arriving late on parade. "Where have you been?"

"Sure I've only been as far as the NAFFI Corporal"

"You've been to the NAFFI?"

In the NAFI

"Sure am'nt I only after telling you that?"

Frustrated he shouted at me to get fell in to a chorus of now sniggering men. As we marched off I decided to play cat and mouse with him by swinging both arms in unison, and deliberately marching out of step. Bringing the squad to a halt he ordered me to wipe the smile from my face, fall out and to stand at attention by the side of the parade ground until teatime.

Next time I fell foul of our instructor was during our very first pay parade. The Flight Sergeant in charge of the pay parade stood us at ease facing a table containing the monies for distribution. Our Corporal mouthed a monologue about the procedures we were to follow when called to collect our pay. As the names were called, we were to come to attention state our "last three numbers, Flight Sergeant" then march to the table. We were *not to salute* as the paying officer was not a commissioned officer. My mind was elsewhere whilst waiting my turn in the roll call. I picked up the drift of the outlined instructions from my predecessors. At the sound of my name I was jolted back to the proceedings. I decided to add my own special touch to the proceedings:

"OK Serge." Which brought a roar of disbelief from the Corporal:

"What do you think this is? Get fell back in line you 'orrible little man and wait your turn until the last".

Deflated I returned to the ranks questioning my error, by whispering from the corner of my mouth from the man next to me, who informed me:

"You're supposed to say Flight Sergeant"

That explained it. I thought they were saying *right* Sergeant.

Paying attention was then not one of my strong points as evident on a warm sunny evening. We'd returned to the billets after meals to find each bed contained a small piece of white cloth, four by six inches. The cloth was sectioned by red stripes about two inches apart. We were making our beds and readying ourselves for a night on the town, when our Corporal entered, informally he requested us to gather around: "I'm going to show you how to clean your rifles".

Hearing that as usual I paid scant attention for I'd played with my rifle long enough to know how to carry out such a simple task. I didn't wish to be distracted from readying myself for a night out. Concluding his demonstration he instructed everyone to clean their rifles. Although I had spent considerable time playing with my toy I'd failed to notice that the piece of string containing metal at one end had two loops on the opposite end. This piece of apparatus was known as a Pull-Through. The end loop was for use by the armour in the event of a blockage in the barrel.

To dislodge obstructions he would use a hooked metal rod to engage the end loop.

I removed the Pull-through and small capsule of oil from the compartment in the butt of the rifle, inserted the piece of red lined oil soaked cloth into the end loop at the of the string. Removing the bolt from the breach I slid the metal end down the barrel of the upturned rifle. Wrapping the string around my fist I pulled once, then again with greater effort but to no avail. Passing the rifle over to the adjacent Irishman:

"Will ye just hold the butt while I pull"?

Our Corporal's face lit up with amusement at the sight of us engaged in a tug-of-war across the bed with little success. Finally with an air of self confidence:

"Give it here, what are they feeding you Irish on?" Wrapping the Pull--through around his hand:

"One clean pull". He tried to demonstrate, but nothing, he tried still harder.... Still no movement. A grin spread across my face, I was beginning to warm to this. With a hint of sarcasm: "What, may I ask did you put in this rifle?"

"The piece of cloth which was on me bed".

He now entered the spirit of my game, as did the on looking men. He smirked as he enquires if I had put the whole piece of cloth (six by two) in the rifle. By now I was enjoying showing off in front of an audience. The cloth was meant to be torn in two.

"I suppose you put it in the armours loop the last loop?"

I pretended surprise and smiled: "Was there another loop?"

Laughter from the men brought the game to an abrupt end. The angered Corporal instructed me to follow him. Still holding the rifle bolt in my hand I was led into the presence of a Sergeant Freeman. The Corporal reported:

"This young man appears to think training is one big joke"

Mischievously I enjoyed pushing the boundaries by I tossing the bolt up and down in my hand. Now I've hooked the Sergeant into my game. "Stand to attention laddie"

Deliberately and calmly I tossed the bolt higher, let it drop to the ground and lazily stooped to pick it up. The Sergeant was not amused:

"Send this man to do fatigues in the Cookhouse until 22.00 hours tonight".

On I returning to my fellow trainees, they gathered around eager to learn what had happened. Totally unaware of the Corporal's presence behind me, I related my encounter with the Sergeant: "Didn't that silly fecken Sergeant only give me cookhouse duties for tonight." The men's faces kept willing me to look around. When I did the Corporal had a triumphant smile as he beckoned me back to the Sergeant. On hearing the account of my reaction to his punishment: "A/C Rice, I am placing you under close arrest for insubordination." The Sergeant ordered the two nearest men forward: "You two will act as escorts and will accompany Rice to the Guardroom, Corporal march them away." Only then did the full gravity of the situation sink in; I'd let it get way out of control. "Ah sure what's wrong with you lot, can't yah take a joke? Have ye no sense of fun a tall?" "Escort, accused, quick march" ordered the Corporal. Still protesting:

"Sure I won't be needin an escort, I know me way to the Guardroom".

As the four of us made our way along the road I kept darting in and out of the line trying to avoid the shame of being seen under close arrest.

Sat on the wooden bed in the cell, with the slanting rays of the sun streaming through the barred windows, I pondered on how in heck I'd landed up there. My main disappointment was having missed a night out with the boys.

A night in the cells failed to put a damper on my mischievous spirits. The following morning under two escorts I was quickly marched to the Camp Headquarters for trial by the Commanding

Officer (CO). The speed of the Sergeant's orders I found confusing, as I wasn't yet quiet fully alert for his quick fire orders:

"Quick march, right turn, left turn, stand at ease, stand easy, accused, hat off",

Bemused I failed to keep up with the pace of the orders.

"Please Serge, can't you take it a little slower?"

"Quiet boy" and with a look of sheer disbelief, just carried on in the same vein as he opens the door to the CO's office. "Escort, accused and witness, attention, right turn, quick march, left turn, halt, right turn."

The intended result of the orders failed as the two escorts and witness were left facing the CO, one move behind the others I ended up with my back to him. The order for me to "about turn" sounded as though it came through gritted teeth. To put it mildly the C.O. was somewhat agitated as he proceeded to read from the charge sheet. I confirmed my name, rank, and the last three of my serial number. He requested the witness, the Corporal to state the evidence of the charge. "Sir, at seventeen thirty hours on the second of June I..." At this stage of the proceedings I could not contain my awe and amusement at the drama unfolding. Grinning, I lean forward to see the Corporal's face, I was fascinated by his cockney accent. Once again I appeared to be pulling the strings. Even the CO looked exasperated: "What in heavens name is it you find so amusing young man?" "Sure doesn't he speak awfully funny?

I soon sobered up with the promise of spending a week in the cells if I failed to shape up. Having no defence I was found guilty as charged and awarded seven days *jankers* (confinement to barracks). The punishment, and the promise of being put back in the cells if I failed to shape up had the desired effect on me, for now.

Only one incident marred the rest of my basic training. This occurred when I attacked a fellow for being rude to me. The men present pulled me off and appeared surprised at my complete loss of control. When asked the reason for my attack on a fellow trainee my response brought a look of incredulity. The fellow had sworn at me, telling me "to f*** off"

The final days of rehearsal for our passing out parade and inspection were tinged with excitement at the thought of two weeks leave, before being directed to our respective trade training units.

With little option I had placed on record my Father's address as next of kin, I needed to keep up the pretence of having a place of residence. Taking up the Father's earlier invite I informed him I was coming "home" on leave it never giving it a thought on how he might view it. It was my only cover.

Our passing out parade went like no other. On completion of our display and inspection we awaited the standard C. O.' s address of farewell and best wishes for the future: "Men, To-day's display (long pause, trying to find the words) was lousy. You will return again in one week's time with a much-improved performance. That week will come off your leave". We marched away shocked and dejected at losing a whole week's leave. This had never happened before. I vowed I'd have my two weeks leave and hang the consequences. Any fears I had of running away had evaporated, knowing the threat of violence and ridicule no longer existed.

I returned to Dublin hoping to find a familiar place where people spoke like me and to feel a sense of belonging. Like a stray cat I moved in on the family and took whatever was offered. Lacking a sense of gratitude I thus retained my independence as a human being. The time had long passed for me to form a relationship with anyone, let alone a member of this well-meaning family.

It was the only place on offer at that time.

At my failure to return to my new unit an official letter arrived to inform me I would be considered AWOL (absent without leave) should I fail to return forthwith, without a valid reason. I ignored the letter and the Father advised me it was best to stay, as there was no future in what I was doing in the Forces. For the first time in my life I was given well meaning advice, not orders or instructions, which I followed. Two men from the British Embassy visited the house and tried to persuade me to return to my unit.

I derived a degree of pleasure laughing and telling them in none too polite term what they could do, knowing as long as I remained in Ireland no one could touch me.

Once again I started work in Dublin, this time at a foundry making heavy industrial equipment such as manhole covers. It left me covered from head to foot in dust and grime at the end of each working day. The mounting cloths washing for May, the Father's partner and daily scrubbing to remove the fine particles of dust from my skin proved too much for me to continue in the job. The Father soon found me another job at an engineering works. I fail to recall what it entailed, but by then I felt very much a lone stray in the city, deeply unsettled and just drifted from day to day. Without a sense of belonging; the call of the pack was too strong for me to ignore.

Without a conscious sense of direction I headed north, intent on resuming the only life where I felt safe understood and belonged. Arrested on arrival by the Military Police by arrangement, I was at last happy knowing I was going *home* to England. As a stray, I had arrived at the Rice' for a short few weeks stay, and as such left without a backward glance, regrets or goodbyes never to see them again.

My punishment for being AWOL was to serve three weeks detention in the cells of the Basic Training Station. This I hardly considered a punishment as I enjoyed some fun times with my jailers. One Policeman appeared to enjoy his work by taunting prisoners.

Whilst overseeing a prisoner scrubbing the floor the he first winked at me, and then kicked the water bucket over. The prisoner's rush of anger subsided just as fast as it arose, which brought a smirk of satisfaction to the cop's face. The same Policeman was later to pay me the finest complement I'd had up to that moment. He'd expressed admiration for the way I cheerfully accepted each form of punishment dished out to me and that nothing appeared to damped my spirits. He would never understand how good it felt knowing I was a better man than he was.

I went on to complete my trade training and was posted to RAF Cranwell Flying Training School to work in the Officers Mess, waiting on tables and cleaning their living quarters. My behaviour was still a long way off from being acceptable to my fellow men. Quick to anger I resorted to violent attacks when slighted in any way.

A resolution to the problem presented itself more by accident than design. I'd started to attend the Gym in the evenings to begin weight training in the hope of attaining a Charles Atlas body. Flight Lieutenant Rutter the boxing coach spotted me working out on the heavy punch bag and persuaded me to take up boxing, I didn't require much persuading. The prospect of legally venting my anger on others was indeed enticing and so promptly joined the Station boxing team.

This was my way of attaining respect from my compatriots by indulging in beating up others in a sport. Always conscious I was different, both within and outside the Forces, although in the latter to a lesser extent.

An incident that reinforced the difference happened on a night out with the boys in the local town of Grantham. There was a sign outside a pub stating boldly, "No Irish or dogs allowed." Not wishing to rock the boat I tried to dissuade the other fellows entering by telling them that the Landlord's wishes should be respected.

Church parades proved somewhat of a puzzle to me. The arrival of the Padre the was followed by the Parade Commander giving the Order:

"Fall out Roman Catholics and Jews"

Accordingly we fell out to the edge of the parade ground but still heard the full text of the sermon and prayers. The prayers and message in the sermon differed little from that which I had grown up with. The service completed we were ordered to fall back into the ranks. In time there were more *Catholics and Jews* fell out than those fell back in on the order to do so. Those missing would sneak back to their billets thus avoiding the dress inspection that followed. Soon I began to box as a lightweight (nine and a half stone) and could alternate between Southpaw (left-handed) and orthodox style. I'd trained with Brin Jones a Southpaw who boxed for Wales. There was also a professional heavyweight, Johnnie Appey whom I'd sparred with intent on learning the art of avoiding his punches whilst he worked on his speed. Jones taught me to slowly move my leading hand in a circular motion until my opponent began to follow the hand movement. Then to quickly move the hand out to the side, with his vision diverted for that split second; strike hard and fast with my other hand.

When Johnnie and I trained he pulled his punches to avoid hurting me, whilst I moved fast to help speed his movements. Unable to resist employing my newfound trick on him as soon as he glanced at my decoy fist, I smacked him right in the gob. From the look of disbelief and anger in his eyes his hurt registered that was the signal for me to skip through the ropes and run.

With a few fights under my belt Flt/Lt Rutter considered I was ready to be selected to represent a RAF team against a US Air Force team at Grantham Town Hall. Mine was the last fight on the bill, matched against an A2C Leonard, a tall lean fellow. By contrast I was of a short (five-foot six/seven) and stocky build which belied my nine and a half stone. During the preceding bouts the shouting for blood, the cheering and jeering from the spectators only served to fire up the worst in me.

Leonard proved to be the more skilful and polished boxer as he showed off his skills by picking me off with jabbing punches as he danced around the ring. He bloodied my nose and inflicted a cut above my eye. By the end of the first round I must have looked a sorry sight. Seeing Officers in evening dress smoking cigars and smiling fuelled my rage. The second round was going the way of the first when I heard jeering laughter from an American voice shout: "Knock a smile on his face."

Furthered encouraged to show off his skills Leonard became careless that by bouncing off the ropes which resulted in him landing close to my fist. With every ounce of strength I struck him hard on the jaw, and as he clung to me for support I delivered a further vicious punch before walking away. I didn't hear the cheering nor did I turn around. He had to be lifted from the ring. There was no feeling of elation only disgust.

That win made me something of a hero in the eyes in my comrades and I received a degree respect from officers.

I continued with my training, but when my trainers talked enthusiastically about preparing for my next fight they were shocked to hear:

"That was my last fight in a ring, I'm not a performing monkey for the amusement of anyone."

Service life agreed with me and some aspects were not unlike my school days when it came to Bank holidays, Christmas or annual leaves. At such times I always volunteered for duty, thus allowing me to enjoy the peace, quiet and less taxing duties on an almost empty camp. Christmas day we had a wonderful dinner waited on by the Officers. When the men returned from the four yearly Grants (bank holidays Whit sun, Easter, August and Christmas) I would enjoy a long lie-in and the use of all the facilities the camp had to offer.

At weekends buses lined up on the Parade Ground to take those in receipt of a thirty-six or forty-eight hour passes to their home towns throughout the UK. On my weekend off I took potluck by hopping on a bus not knowing where I'd land up. At each destination I would check in at the local YMCA or a bed and breakfast lodgings, and frequent the pubs and dancehalls in the area.

After work at weekends, I would visit the local towns in the company of the men some dressed in uniform.

One Saturday night A fellow Airman, Jim Dinsdale and I had left a dance at Newark Town to join the crowd awaiting busses. A local fellow was using foul language, which left me outraged: "Would you mind not using that language in front of girls?"

He moved menacingly towards me: "What are you going to do about it"?

"Never mind what I'm going to do, and please don't raise your hands to me."

He paid scant heed to my advice. Handing my overcoat and hat to Jim I didn't have long to wait for his attack. I derived a great deal of pleasure of beating the hell out of him. Afterwards I felt ashamed at what I had done as he was untrained to defend himself. His friends however got their own back knocking me to the ground and giving me a good kicking. In the melee I heard the sound of a police whistle and felt myself being picked up by a large American Airman who then ran with me up a quite ally. When I got back to camp I was a little the worst for wear, bruised and watch broken.

It appeared that trouble was destined to find me and I had yet to discover how to steer clear. A fact which was re-enforced by events which took place in the officer's mess bar, where I was in sole charge on a quiet weekday evening. For an officer to order a drink he would enter his name and bar-number, plus his order on one of the pads on the bar counter. Handing over the signed order I'd serve him and place the chit on a spike holder. These chits were collected the following morning where details and costs were entered in the respective officers bar account books. Flt. Lt. May was a test pilot at the Training School. I knew him as a very generous and friendly man.

On entering the bar he placed his order and gave me ten shillings to buy myself some drinks. Part of my duties was to keep the petty cash and enter cash sales in a book. Visiting officers paid cash, not having a bar book. The evening was quiet in the bar I decided to enjoy a glass of whiskey, the details and price I entered in the cashbook. It was a long time until closing and with little or no customers I had another drop of the hard stuff. As my partaking of the hard stuff increased, the entries in the cashbook became laborious and illegible. I became a little the worst for wear and failed to notice the bar start to fill up with customers and orders were coming too thick and fast. Then beer ran short and I had to tap another barrel that I make a complete mess of. With the beer spewing out all over me I decided, that's it! I'd had enough and in response to the persistent demands for service I became incapable of providing any further service:

"Ah go on and help yourselves I'm off to bed."

I still had the presence of mind to fetch my hat, which was in the staff rest/dining room. The door was locked and whoever was in there was not acknowledging my request to let me in. Required to wear my hat at all times out doors, so intent on fetching it I attacked the door with my fists. Smashing the panel I place my eye to the opening:

"I can see you. Ah come on now open the door, I want me hat." When I failed to secure the hat I staggered off to bed and fell into a deep sleep, to be woken some hours later by a policeman asking for the keys to the bar. I passed them over and continued my drunken sleep.

The following morning I was charged with dispensing a large portion of the bar stock without properly accounting, damaging property and being under the influence of alcohol whilst on duty. Once again I found myself in an all too familiar situation. The charges are considered serious enough to warrant being referred to the CO.

My punishment was to spend a period of detention in the Station Guardroom cells.

It was late 1952 when Bill Gaskill, a fellow Batman/Waiter asked why I spent my leaves and Bank Holidays on the camp. Didn't I have a home to go to? Being too ashamed to admit I didn't, I excused my self by telling him it was too far to travel. Rejecting his invitation to visit his home for Christmas I explained there could be no better way to spend it than by being on duty. It wasn't until we both had forty-eight hour weekends pass did I accepted his second invitation to visit Co. Durham.

That visit ended my forays around the UK, for I'd found a warmth and friendliness in the surrounding mining villages of Co. Durham I'd not experienced anywhere to date. It was the beginning of a love affair with the area and the people, resulting in all my weekend and holiday countrywide travels coming to an end. Wearing uniform proved to be very effective for hitch hiking from Lincolnshire whenever I didn't have a rail pass. To hear a Geordie accent and hop on a local bus with its rich smell of miners Condor Slice pipe tobacco were the first signal that I was truly 'home'. When paying my fare I tried to speak quietly for fear my accent would draw attention, as few if any outsiders visited these parts.

Many of the working class people lived in what would now be described as dire poverty, but to me it went unnoticed because of a richness that cannot remotely compare with the more materially affluent. Doors weren't locked; neighbours knew and supported one another. The mining villages of Stanley, Crook, West Auckland and many more appeared never to sleep. The night sky was lit up with the twinkling lights of the pits, where men worked shifts round the clock. There was no shortage of activities for members of the Armed Forces, who had free access to the miners' clubs and the Miners Institutes where beer was cheaper than in pubs.

Initially I stayed at Bill's house, he had three sisters and two younger brothers. Sadly, I'm shamed to admit that I was unconscious of the unwarranted intrusion my presence must have caused them. Frances, the eldest sister and I became friends and together we went to village dances. At one such dance she became involved in a conversation with a man she knew. I discreetly made myself scarce. Frances later asked me why I had disappeared. My explanation of not wanting to be in the way if she wished to be with the fellow, somewhat puzzled her. In time I was to discover most men were jealous over women, this I failed to understand and am still puzzled.

It was at a village dance I discovered that there was some merit to being Irish.

Whilst talking to a girl at a village hall I overheard one of her friends saying:

"I just love his accent; I could listen to him all night."

It was in the latter part of my third year's service that I became aware of changes around me. Men I knew were leaving, having completed their compulsory two years National Service. Bill became engaged and other men were getting married. The realisation dawned on me that my time was running out and I wondered what was to become of me I thought: "I can't leave the service, where am I to go in this strange land?" There seemed no option but to apply to extend my service period. Before I submitted the application I knew there now had to be a change in my attitude and approach to service life.

Enlisting in evening education classes and involving myself in trade training I intended to become a Mess Steward. In my spare time I trained hard at a number of sports. With eighteen months of my service engagement remaining I'd passed exams in basic Math, English and General Knowledge, and also graduated to Acting Corporal. Despite these successes my superiors felt I still lacked certain qualities to warrant full promotion to Corporal. On the sports front I succeeded in representing my Station at Basketball, cross-country, track and road running.

Cross Country

As a result of my promotion I was posted to another RAF Station in Lincolnshire, but I continued to spend my leaves in my adopted home area of Co. Durham. On one of my leaves I attended a dance at the Bishop Auckland Town Hall accompanied by local acquaintances. One of them, a local lad, serving in the RAF, Sid Blackmore, had a crush on one of two girls dancing together. He knew her, as Joan Lyons, too shy to speak to her, he enlisted my help by asking me to agreed by splitting them up. The other girl was a beautiful blue eyed, petite brunette and looked to be way out of our league.

I apologised for intruding and introduced myself as Paddy and explained I was helping my friend to meet Joan. She said her name was Jean Dixon, but I got cold feet and I tried to excuse myself by saying I could not do that dance. In a shy but encouraging voice she responded:

"That's O.K. let's just try."

I took her dainty hand in my rough grasp and placed my arm around her slim waist.

I can't recall much about the dance except sheer bliss, I must have been floating on air. The rest of the evening we spent together, *talking*.

That is to say I did most of the talking, trying to find out as much as I could about her. She said very little only to answer to my queries in a quiet tone of voice. She was a good listener. Her very presence stirred in me an overwhelming protective feeling towards her. This girl I wished to shower with worldly goods. She was eighteen and I twenty-one and truly smitten

Jean @ 18

Me @ 21

CHAPTER SEVEN

Someone Cares

Some inexplicable power had taken over my life and given it purpose. There was a compelling urge for me to spend as much time in the company of Jean as possible. Leaves and weekend passes were spent in Co. Durham. Determined to maintain contact with her I hopped on a Friday afternoon bus from Bishop Auckland to West Auckland intent on meeting her by *accident.* The plan was to appear to be making my way to the bus stop on the opposite side of the road to her place of work. Time seemed to stand still as I waited for the sound of the five o'clock building siren, the signal for the workforce to pour from the clothing factory. On the signal I walked some distance from the bus stop before retracing my steps as the workers started to cross the road. It was difficult to contain my excitement as I approached my beloved Jean as she neared the bus stop. A hint of a smile lit up her lovely face: "What are *you* doing here?"

"Just thought I'd familiarise myself with the area. I'm on my way to Bishop Auckland."

We passed the time with small talk, and just as the bus approached I made a clumsy, garbled plea: "There's this film on at the cinema in Bishop on Saturday night. Would you do me the honour?" To my joy she accepted the invitation and hurried arrangements were made.

From that moment our courtship began. Letters were exchanged and I found myself hitchhiking up North every free weekend to be with her. Sweet ration coupons were hoarded to purchase her favourite confectionary, a box of Panes Poppets.

When at last she invited me to her home I was confident she cared about me, and the prospects of meeting her family bore no fears. She lived in what was known as *The Square*, an enclosure of terraced houses built around a once grassy green, the grass had long since vanished. Now the area was compacted with the ashes from numerous grates, and in the winter the ashes sizzled as they soaked up the damp patches of earth. Jean's was an end house, the one break in the centre of a facing row. Unlike the countless others the back entrance was to the side. Visitors would be greeted by the women folk with the words: "Dina bring yur clats (clots or mud) in 'ere".

It was easy to see where Jean got her good looks. Her Mother's smile was warmly and welcoming: "You must be Paddy, Jean's told me so much about you."

Immediately I felt at ease as she took me under her wing, deliberately setting out to make me feel at home. This was as surprising as it was unexpected. Why would any Mother want a young fellow the likes of me, so lacking in social graces, to be going out with their daughter? It also puzzled me how she managed to be immaculately turned out in addition to possessing a great sense of humour. This in contrast to her husband, who was a quiet, amiable man who spent his spare time as a bookie's runner and liked taking a drink at the nearby *Locomotive*.

He had once worked in the mines, until an injury cut short that career. Now he was employed as a porter at the nearby railway station. Jean was the second of three grown-up girls; two boys who were still at school completed the family unit. The eldest Gladys, had married and moved on, while Jean and her sister Joyce worked at the local clothing factory after finishing school at fourteen, helping to boost the family's meagre income.

The family was crowded into the two small bedrooms.

Downstairs the front room was reserved for visitors and was kept spick and span as was the custom in working class households. Jean's Mum, Lily's pride and joy resided in the parlour, a lovingly polished piano.

Lily Dixon and Band

Hearing her play, no one could doubt that a trained musician was at work. Beautiful in both looks and temperament, Lily earned pin money playing with a local band, money that both provided to keep her fashionably dressed as well as boosting with the family finances. At the *Loco* at weekends, Lily would oblige with requests for tunes, and such evenings often ended up in a fabulous singsong But the most industrious room of the house was the kitchen with it's blazing coal fire, connected to an oven in which most of the family's meals were cooked. Leaning against the oven was a *bleezer* (a curved metal shield-like object with a handle), which was used to draw the fire. A large black kettle squatted on the fire or hot plate, ever ready to infuse a welcome brew of tea. In winter house bricks were heated in the oven, wrapped in cloth and made good substitutes for hot water bottles as bed warmers.

A well-worn couch faced the fireplace with the all-purpose table in the middle of the room abutted to its rear. Against the back wall was the wooden dresser, while in the rear corner of the room a cold water tap dribbled into the Belfast sink. A Galvanised tin bath hung on the back of the pantry door next to the clothes mangle, beside a back door, which was seldom locked.

A visit to the lavatory meant crossing a path at the rear of the house, which on Mondays was festooned with the family's laundry. As sheets and clothes blew in the breeze they wafted in their wake the unmistakeable scent of Lifebuoy soap.

Each time I entered the *Square* by the narrow side street off the main road the breathtaking terrible beauty of the place almost overwhelmed me. There were usually happy, soot streaked faced children's voices to be heard as they chased their dogs or played with discarded old prams. The houses portrayed a happy childlike crayon drawing, with individually coloured front doors, and each with a window upstairs and down. The stunted chimneys puffed out varying shades of smoke from very fine white to deep black. The front pathways to the bunched up houses were fastidiously scrubbed weekly, and the summer-whitewashed windowsills were respectably spotless.

Although the place is long since wiped from the map, every small detail is indelibly etched forever in my mind's eye. These warm sweet-loving memories represented my very first taste of family life and would become the sure foundations for my own future family. Jean's close knit extended family welcomed me. Her youngest brother Tommy was intrigued to learn that I'd boxed and we enjoyed many sparing sessions. Soon he enrolled in the local boxing club and went on to represent England internationally. Accepted by all as part of the family I was accorded the couch in the front room on my regular overnight visits.

Jean made me feel safe and accepted and instinctively I trusted her. She radiated tenderness, life-giving warmth and love. It was not long before I knew I wished to spend the rest of my life with her. Without considering our circumstances I asked her to marry me, a proposal that caused her some surprise: "I'm only eighteen! Far too young. What will my Mom say?" I tried to joke: "I'm not asking to marry your Mum. It's you I want to marry, I'll wait until you and your Mum feel you're old enough to accept me."

" I like you so much Paddy. But you're different from anybody I've ever known. Let's take time to get to know and understand each other better".

She found it strange when I insisted on us visiting her Grandmother with flowers and chocolate, she lived alone just a few doors down from her. I failed to understand how people could take their closest relations for granted: "You're so lucky to have a proper family. It's what I've always dreamed of and now I'm wishing to have one of my own."

"Don't you have Grandparents?" Always the positive thinker: "No, but then I'm lucky in that

I don't have anyone to lose, and I'll be spared the awful pain you must have to suffer when loved ones die."

These words would come back to haunt me with a vengeance. I'd told her of my sister Phyllis but nothing of my 'Jesuit Fathers' type upbringing.

"What about your sister Phyllis?"

"I didn't grow up with her and didn't meet her 'till I was seventeen."

"You're strange." That phrase I would come to hear often repeated in the years to come. Jean decided not to pursue the matter, perhaps she'd responded unwittingly to my body language warning her to tread carefully.

Over the next year our relationship blossomed, we spent every moment together, often babysitting Jean's elder sister's first born. Sometimes we went to the cinema or danced at the Town Hall. It was at one of these dances that she first observed the uncouth, uneducated side of her partner. In future years she would cringe with embarrassment and whisper: "Oh Paddy please don't show me up."

For instance while dancing with her one night I was horrified to see a big strapping fellow beating the daylights out of a little runt on the dance floor.

To my amazement everyone appeared blind to this outrageous spectacle while bystanders ignored the fracas as they nonchalantly moved away from the hapless victim. Jean, sensing the anger welling up in me, grasped my hand tightly: "It's got nothing to do with us Paddy." "I'm sorry, but it's just not fair, is it"? Unable to contain my anger, it exploded as I waded into the bully. To this day I fail to comprehend how I managed to throw that huge fellow down the stairs and out of the hall. For my efforts I ended up with my shirt torn and blood stained from a bloodied nose. Somehow Jean managed to clean me up and hid the torn shirt with deft fingers thus giving a semblance of respectability.

I'd yet to learn how to steer clear of trouble even on camp. As the senior of two Corporals in charge of the Officer's Mess staff, I reported directly to a civilian manager, an ex-Army major called Mr. Hayhurst. Instinctively I rebelled at having to accept orders from a civilian. Twice my substantive Corporal's promotion came through from RAF HQ only to have it rejected by Hayhurst. It was the unenviable duty of my C.O. to explain to me why my promotion had been rejected. The C. O. asked the Manager to leave us before proceeding to outline the case:

"Hayhurst says that every morning you report for duty with a sullen look and rude manner. I'd like to see you making amends. Perhaps you could enter the office with a polite smile, with the words:

"What can I do for you to-day, sir. Now I'm going to call the manager back, while you leave this office. Wait outside 'til I bid you enter, then we'll rehearse your future greetings." I knock and enter; Hayhurst looks up from his desk:

"Yes. What can I do for you?" "Nothin!" (nothing) The CO exploded with exasperation:

"Look here Corporal. You approach the Manager as if you're picking a fight. With that attitude you will never be considered for promotion to a substantive NCO."

"I can't help the way I feel sir". "Good God man. Can't help? Life's a game and you'd better get and learn to play your part correctly if you wish to progress". With that he stormed out. Hayhurst proceeded to outline the changes required if I was to work successfully with him in order to gain a promotion I sorely needed if I was to create a secure career base before embarking on marriage.

To prove my determination to shape up I applied to attend the N.C.O's Training School located in the West Midlands.

This course was attended by a number of acting Corporals and Leading Aircraftmen and an Acting Sergeant who was designated Senior Man. His responsibilities were to march us to and from classrooms and meals, not dissimilar to basic training. We were all billeted in one Nissan hut and each supplied with a rifle. The main training subjects were military law and responsibilities of N. C. Os.' in relation to their subordinates.

Determined to prove to myself I could become a better than average N.C.O. by applying one hundred per cent to all given tasks. It was, therefore, unfortunate that one morning, I'd reverted to type. Dressed immaculately, I'd hoped to be early lined up on parade for the days allotted tasks. On going to retrieve my rifle from the stack in the centre of the room, it was gone. Having spent the previous evening cleaning and polishing the weapon I was now forced to wait and accept the lone unclean rifle. I trundled outside the last to join the waiting group, muttering choice expletives aimed at whoever had stolen my weapon. One upset man chirped up as he stepped out of line and trusts a rifle into my hand: "Quit moaning. Here's your bloody rifle".

Totally losing control I punched him squarely in the midriff. Unfortunately I was still holding the rifle resulting in the foresight guard of the weapon nicking his eyebrow drawing blood. The Acting Sergeant quietened things down, and nothing more was made of the incident. But later I failed to understand why my fellow would-be N. C. Os. cold-shouldered me. Queering their attitude, one of the group suggested that, I'd acted disgracefully towards a fellow airman. This left me puzzled, had I not punished a cheat? Why can't they see the injustice of their behaviour?

"That guy needed sorting out. No body walks over me."

In spite of that, I'd passed the course with flying colours and received the promotion I'd strived so hard for with Mr. Hayhurst's endorsement. As a full corporal my rank and position became more financially secure. It enhanced my marriage prospects and guaranteed a married quarter would be available for me and my would be bride.

A year had passed since I'd proposed to Jean. An engagement ring was bought and accepted, but my happiness was somewhat marred by one nagging question that would haunt me for years. Over and over again I would query of Jean, well knowing my social shortcomings:

Corporal

"What ever was it that made you accept me? I'm nothing better than a lone stray mongrel." Her answer was always the same, patient, kind and gentled with compassion. "Because I love you, Paddy that's it."

Can it be that simple I constantly asked myself?

With my return to duties in the Officers' Mess I found it impossible to keep up the pretence of being polite to the Mess Manager and reverted to my original offhand attitude. Asked if I had been acting the part, I confirmed that I had done so sorely to achieve my objective. Why continue to be a hypocrite?

In the year of our engagement I'd spent both Christmas and New Years with Jean's family, and was delighted to be accepted as "Weir Paddy". But despite their genuine attempts to enfold me in their family circle, something within me felt this to be false. Would I always hover on the out side looking on as an interested observer? The fact was the whole thing was alien to my coarsely reared self.

At family gatherings in the local pub on Christmas Eve I listened avidly to animated conversations about bygone Christmases, and at the stroke of midnight at New Year's Eve I went *First Footing* with other male members of the family and friends. It was heady stuff. A year previously I had been a stranger, yet welcomed with open arms at the houses in Jean's neighbourhood. It was amazing to receive drink and silver coins after wishing them a Happy New Year, feeling overwhelmed at their largesse.

Our wedding which was arranged for the twenty-fourth of September 1955. Sure I knew my beloved was twenty years old but it never entered my head to ask the date of her birthday, and strangely she didn't ask about mine, about three years older. I'd yet to become accustomed to celebrating ones birthday. I must have been strangely non-communicative about my upbringing and how I had subconsciously suppressed the memories of years in institutions, only much, much, later did I understand.

At base camp there was a requirement for an N.C.O to perform a weekend prisoner escort duty, collecting an airman from civil police custody in Newcastle.

This required the unpleasant task for the station Administration Warrant Officer to detail an off duty Corporal and airman for escort duty over a weekend.

The W.O. got wind of my impending marriage to a girl in Co. Durham and considered he was doing me a favour by choosing me as a suitable candidate. He also decreed that I would be accompanied by a Scottish airman who was serving a C.B. (confinement to barrack) punishment, rather than detail an off duty colleague. Issued with railway warrants, handcuffs, and truncheon, I listened carefully to my superior officer's commands: Jock and I were to collect the prisoner and return him to the custody of the RAF police at the camp Guardroom.

It was late Friday evening when we arrived at Newcastle Rail Station and easy to convince myself that it was too late to make the return journey in the dark, perhaps handcuffed to the prisoner. With this in mind I floated the idea that Jock might wish to visit his home. The young Scot was overjoyed at the prospects of spending two nights at home in Glasgow, while I of course spent time with my beloved Jean.

Sunday morn I met the young Scot at Newcastle Railway Station as arranged and made our way to the Police Station where we were not greeted with undiluted joy.

It appeared we were meant to collect our prisoner and return with him same evening to our unit. The tone of the Policeman said it all: "Where the hell have you been? We were expecting you on Friday evening. Your C.O. will be receiving a very strong letter of complaint."

My lame excuses about it being dark and unsafe for an over night journey fell on deaf ears. Privately I'd thought that "Trouble" would make me a good middle name, but I wasn't duly concerned, as I arrogantly believed I could work the system. The rest of our assignment was completed without incident.

The following morning I received instructions to report to the Admin Office and was formally charged by the Warrant Officer with failing to carry out orders as instructed. I'd chosen to remain silent, except when asked if I had anything to say, I replied "not guilty". At my hearing by my C.O. when invited to present my defence, I explained that as an NCO I believed I was expected I use my initiative. I explained the issuing of handcuffs and a truncheon implied there might be a serious risk by travelling with a prisoner on public transport after dark. With that in mind I'd therefore sought overnight accommodation for the escort and myself. At this point the C.O. cut me short and barked at the W.O. "Did you, or did you not, give the Corporal detailed times and dates as to when, where and how he was to collect and to return the prisoner."

"Well sir I told him to collect..." Interrupted by the C.O. "It's a simple question sir; you either did or did not give him clear written instructions, leaving him in no doubt as to his orders. Well?" "No Sir." "Very well Warrant Officer, you can leave. Case dismissed. However Corporal Rice you and I know you are lying through your back teeth.

Be warned don't you ever pull a stunt like that again."

The pangs of guilt that I'd felt for the Warrant Officer soon passed, I'd won.

On a glorious September Saturday the 24th in 1955, Jean and I became one in marriage at St. Philomena's Catholic Church, just across the road from her home.

Wedding/1

I'd only had eyes for her, in a beautiful white dress, holding a spray of red roses. Entering a fresh clean New World where the sweet scent of roses perfumed the air. Hence forth red roses would forever hold great significance for me. So happy to make the vows to love, honour and cherish in sickness and health, unaware that in some distant future all my physical and mental powers would be challenged to the limit to hold true to these promises.

AS we left the church I felt literally newborn. There would be no looking over my shoulder from whence I had come and the cold cradling of childhood.

It would be decades before I would be jolted out of my wilful amnesia.

Knowing nothing about psychology or the damage I carried within me like a defective gene, I blithely set out on the primrose path of marriage and parenthood brimming with confidence in my own abilities to be a loving husband and the fondest of parents.

The journey would take us to live and work as far a field as Europe, the Far and Middle East, far-flung places for a girl who previously had only briefly visited the local seaside and then cried because she wanted to go home.

Along the way there would be great happiness and substantial achievements for an infant cradled in the cold comfort of Industrial Schools, firstly by nuns then Christian Brothers.

It was as if Ireland, together with those intender nuns and Christian Brothers had never existed. Had I dared look in the dark recesses of my mind I might have wondered *why* I so hated my Irish accent or rarely referred to my early years? It would be decades before I realized, with shocking clarity, the full extent of the lifelong damage that has only been released with the writing of this book. Written in spare moments snatched from caring for my life's companion, attempting to repay in some measure the unconditional love and compassion Jean has ever shown me. Too late for her to comfort me when the pain of recall proved all but overwhelming. Too late to understand and forgive the boorish behaviour that so often puzzled and saddened her. Her unconditional love has been the inspiration for me to fulfil what would appear the impossible dream.

Wedding/2

Postscript:

On the Friday 13th January 2006, I received the following photocopied facts under the Freedom of Information Act 1997 which, is recorded thus:

No in Register: *75462*. Name and No. in Industrial school: *Patrick Charles Rice, 11536.* Where, When, and by whom ordered to be detained: *10/2/34, Dublin District Criminal Court, Judge Cussen.* With what charged: *Receiving Alms i.e. Begging.* General remarks: *Transferred to Kilkenny, Father deserted family. Mother in Regina Colei Hostel, Dublin.* Date of discharge: *7 October 1947.* When admitted: *24 Nov. 1941.* Payment per week: *Nil.* Ultimate Disposal: *To Mother, 4 Florence Street, South Circular Road, Dublin. For employment at Western Hotel S.*

S. Rd. Dublin. Page Boy 10/= p. w.

Note:

I was two years old when I was charged, and ordered to be detained until aged sixteen!

I have never lived with my mother.